LEGAL SYSTEMS
OF SCOTTISH CHURCHES

LEGAL SYSTEMS OF SCOTTISH CHURCHES

Editor
MARJORY A MacLEAN
Depute Clerk
General Assembly of the Church of Scotland

DUNDEE UNIVERSITY PRESS
2009

First published in Great Britain in 2009 by
Dundee University Press
University of Dundee
Dundee DD1 4HN

www.dup.dundee.ac.uk

ISBN 978-1-84586-066-0

No natural forests were destroyed to make this product;
only farmed timber was used and replanted.

British Library Cataloguing-in-Publication Data
A catalogue record for this book is available on request from the British Library.

Typeset by Waverley Typesetters, Fakenham
Printed and bound by CPI Group (UK) Ltd, Croydon, CR0 4YY

CONTENTS

FOREWORD

We are living in a time of increased and increasing regulation. The State appears to reach into and attempt to regulate more areas of public and private life then ever before – presumably in the pursuit of equality and fairness, although sometimes achieving only an unbending uniformity. Society seems more litigious and there is an increased awareness of the rights of the individual and attention to legal process. Against that, one can also encounter a feeling or view that legal process is a complicated and expensive irrelevance preventing a common-sense solution of problems. It is hard not to feel sympathy for elements of these views, although experience as a practising lawyer has sometimes shown me that it is often the lack of a proper discussion or analysis which can make a situation more complicated and less bearable.

The Church of Scotland has for years been regulating its operations with a detailed and rigorous system of laws and regulations to ensure that those involved in the life of the Church as it serves the wider community do so in a system that is fair and consistent. This is equally true for many other churches and denominations. A Church operating such a legal system must be able to demonstrate that it administers its legal system and procedures fairly, consistently and competently, and that persons subject to the provisions and application of that system are treated properly and have the protections they enjoy in the ordinary legal system.

One factor which has been noticeable of late is that as people have become more knowledgeable about their rights and about civil legal process, so there has been an increase in external or independent legal representation in the courts and tribunals of the Church of Scotland. This is not unwelcome; rather, the Church is glad that persons facing legal or administrative proceedings, which may have serious implications for their lives and careers, should have access to good independent advice.

In 2007, the Solicitor of the Church of Scotland and the Depute Clerk to the General Assembly gave seminars for practising lawyers on the Church's legal system and constitution, with particular focus on the provisions of Act III 2001 (discipline of ministers and others). These were very well received by solicitors and advocates and it became clear that many lawyers would find a volume introducing and outlining the law and practice of the Church to be both useful and interesting. It seemed a good opportunity to invite the Scottish Episcopal Church and the Roman Catholic Church, as other Christian denominations in Scotland also with systems of law and procedure, to take the opportunity to set down an outline or at least contribute information about their respective systems. Thus the publication grew to encompass chapters from the Scottish Episcopal Church on its polity, law and governance and its judicial procedures as well as material on Presbyterian governance as evidenced in the Church of Scotland, the various judicial Commissions of the Church of Scotland and its procedure and disciplinary process.

As civil law is constantly changing, so is its effect on organisations such as Churches. Situations which may seem new or altered face many who work and hold positions of responsibility within Churches: ministers and the office-bearers of Kirk Sessions, Presbyteries and their clerks, as well as other denominations' priests, deacons and church lawyers. While those civil law questions are pressing with new force, internal Church law has long formed part of the training of the clergy in each Church, and it is hoped that this book might be easily readable by theology students and the like, who will find the description of their Church familiar but may find it useful to see how the decision making fits together. The text should also be a welcome and useful introduction or source of reference to other people within the Churches who are required to interpret and apply the laws of the Church.

CAROLE HOPE
Convenor of the Legal Questions Committee
of the Church of Scotland

CHAPTER I

PRESBYTERIAN GOVERNANCE

MARJORY A MacLEAN

1.1 Presbyterianism and Reformed Polity

1.1.1 *The Scottish Reformation*

The Scottish Reformation is traditionally dated from 1560, and its chief figure is usually acknowledged as John Knox, who was a collaborator with John Calvin in Geneva. In Scotland the Reformation was not a classically "magisterial" change, because the Crown (Mary Stuart) remained Roman Catholic throughout. The social and cultural change was driven largely by some of the leading noblemen, known as the Lords of the Congregation; thus the Scottish Estates and the Church's early General Assemblies had largely overlapping memberships and worked for the same principles and to the same end.

1.1.2 *Genevan polity*

In Calvin's Geneva, the moral authority of the Reformed Church dominated temporal affairs, and the religious Consistory exercised extensive influence over many areas of civic life. In Calvinist theology, the civil magistrate was viewed as having a positive responsibility for ensuring the promotion of Christian life and teaching, without, however, having control over the Church, and in this respect the Genevan model expected far more than was expected of a Lutheran magistrate.

Perhaps because of this underlying model of the relationship between Church and magistrate, the Reformed understanding of "establishment" of churches emphasises the freedom of the Church to legislate in spiritual affairs without any interference from or supervision by the civil power (see section 1.2 below). The effect is that establishment involving Reformed Churches is generally very different from, say, English Church establishment. The two should not be confused, and it is therefore probably wise not to use the term "established church" loosely in a Scottish context.

1.1.3 Presbyterianism today

During the period of British colonial expansion, the Church of Scotland took Presbyterian church life to many countries. At the end of the colonial era, the Presbyterian Churches in most parts of the former Empire were subject to a process normally referred to as "indigenisation", and became autonomous Reformed Churches. Many remained English speaking, and most became part of the World Alliance of Reformed Churches, of which the Church of Scotland is also a member. The polities of many Presbyterian Churches, especially in Commonwealth countries, are modelled on that of the Church of Scotland, and the tracing of this heritage of belief and practice lies behind the warmth of feeling often directed towards the Scottish Church. An understanding of the law and governance of the Church of Scotland will often be helpful for understanding the polity of those other Churches, though the detailed provisions of the law will differ, and should never be presumed for one from knowledge of another.

1.1.4 Presbyterianism and democracy

Presbyterianism is a form of church governance by a hierarchy of courts. The membership of the courts consists of the spiritual leaders of the Church, being (in the Church of Scotland) the ministers, professional deacons (the Diaconate) and elders of the Church. These three categories listed consist of all who are ordained in the Church, and no one outside that spiritual leadership may be a voting member of any court. It is wrong, but sadly quite common, to hear reference to "lay leadership/ governance" in the Church of Scotland; the phrase fails to recognise the ordination of all elders.

The implication of government by spiritual leaders is that the communicant membership does not ordinarily have any role in determining policy or exercising executive superintendence. However, ideals of transparency and consultation demand that the membership of the Church should be given opportunity to indicate its opinion on important matters, especially policy decisions which will require particular support (eg financial commitment). The final decision in each case, however, remains with the relevant court.

There are three exceptions – situations where a congregation has a deliberative vote – and each exists for particular historical reasons:

- The whole worshipping congregation, including communicant members and adherents, elects the minister. The Presbytery has a veto, and the responsibility of inducting the minister to the charge, but cannot proceed without the majority approval of the congregation. This is the remaining expression of the historic right of the people of a parish to choose and call their pastor.[1]

- The communicant members, in the most common form of congregational constitution, have the responsibility of electing members onto the Congregational Board (the financial board of the congregation responsible for routine temporal affairs), where they serve along with some or all of the elders. This reflects the members' financial responsibilities, particularly emphasised in the Voluntarist tradition of some of the constituent denominations now forming the Church.[2]

- The congregation has a veto over the final disposal of a Church building once used for worship. This probably reflects the recognition of the people's original generosity in providing the asset, and the spiritual and moral interest that might be said to continue to be theirs.[3]

Generally, however, all policy-making and important executive decisions are made by a court of the Church and implemented in its name.

1.2 Spiritual Jurisdiction and the 1921 Settlement

1.2.1 Church and State

Throughout the Church worldwide, Christians profoundly believe that they have a loyalty to God which is higher than any other commitment or duty. From time to time that "ultimate",

---

[1] Act VIII 2003 (as amended) anent Vacancy Procedure.
[2] Act II 1994 anent Model Deeds of Constitution.
[3] Act VII 1995 (as amended) anent Powers Delegated to the Church of Scotland General Trustees.

spiritual, loyalty conflicts with the duty of the citizen to uphold the civil law, and can give rise to crises of conscience and force the individual to take a principled stand which conflicts with the law.

For the Church as a whole, the same kind of difficulty can have more endemic implications. The Church may wish to be able to impose on its members some requirement which is not provided in civil law. (For example, the Church is likely to wish to regard adultery as a disciplinary offence, though it is not a crime in secular law.) The standards of the Church, in other words, may come into conflict with the requirements of the law. For as long as the Church has been an influential institution within civic society, there has been a debate about the need for the Church to have an independent jurisdiction over its members for spiritual purposes – one which is exempt from the scrutiny of the civil law – so that the Church is able to apply its own distinctive standards and requirements.

Various models have come and gone, and some of them prevail in significant denominations today. In the Church of England, for example, there are connections between the policy making of the Church and the law making of Parliament, so that the distinctive rules and regulations of the Church form part of the *corpus* of English Law and are often still confirmed in Parliament itself. In the case of some of the smaller denominations and other faiths in Britain, there is very little sense of a separate spiritual jurisdiction, and the internal rules of the institution have little more status than the internal rules of any large association. The Church of Scotland has a unique relationship with civil law – a relationship which has arisen through a long history of wrestling with the civil magistrate over spiritual affairs.

1.2.2   *The Disruption of 1843*

Between the Reformation of 1560 and the Disruption of 1843, some fragmentation had begun to occur in the Presbyterian Church, often as a result of disputes over issues of religious freedom and the connection between the Church and civic life. In the mid-19th century, a prevailing model of Church–State relations was one which deemed the national Church to be a creature of the State, or of civil legislation. Part of the Church of Scotland resented this model strenuously, pursuing instead an understanding of the Church as jurisdictionally independent of the State in matters of worship, doctrine, church government and discipline.

The culmination of this tension was a major split in the ranks of the Church of Scotland in 1843, the creation of the Free Church of Scotland, and the reluctant severing by the Free Church of the pre-existing relationship of Church and State on their part. This last action gives that sequence of events the name "the Disruption".[4] With the passage of a further half-century, there was a strong desire to re-unite all the strands of Presbyterianism in Scotland; clearly the chief difficulty in achieving the union was the difference in understanding about the legal relationship with the State.

This history is relevant, because still today the heritage of each individual congregation, the way in which it owns heritable property, and the way in which it is governed for temporal purposes, varies according to the Church "strand" from which it derives. It is always worth knowing a little of the history of any congregation before embarking on any legal dealings with it.

1.2.3 The Articles Declaratory and the Church of Scotland Act 1921

Long before the Churches re-united in 1929, it was necessary to find a formula to state the modern relationship of Church and State, and do so in a way that satisfied the consciences of all parties. Long negotiations stretching from 1907 to 1929 found a largely acceptable formula; incorporated it into a constitutional statement (the *Articles Declaratory of the Constitution of the Church of Scotland in Matters Spiritual*[5]); arranged for it to be appended to a piece of civil legislation (the Church of Scotland Act 1921[6]); brought the Act into effect by statutory instrument (in 1926); and used the text as the main element of the constitution of the post-1929 Church for spiritual purposes.[7]

The settlement, which can be found in Articles IV and VI of the Articles, declares the Church to have an independent spiritual jurisdiction which belongs inherently to the Church (ie is not conveyed by any civil, human, authority). The jurisdiction extends to the traditional four areas of worship, doctrine, church

---

[4] See, for example, A C Cheyne, *The Ten Years' Conflict and the Disruption: An Overview* (Edinburgh, 1993) and Lord Rodger of Earlsferry, *The Courts, the Church and the Constitution: Aspects of the Disruption of 1843* (Edinburgh, 2008).

[5] See J L Weatherhead (ed), *The Constitution and Laws of the Church of Scotland* (Edinburgh, 1997), p 159 for the text of the Articles Declaratory.

[6] c 29.

[7] See, for example, D M Murray, *Rebuilding the Kirk: Presbyterian Reunion in Scotland 1909–1929* (Edinburgh, 2000).

government and discipline. Provided that the Church can succeed in arguing that a decision of any of its courts falls entirely into one or more of those categories, there should be no possibility of review of the decision by the civil courts. Decisions which have other elements, or decisions challenged for reasons of process not substance, produce from time to time problematic cases, in which it is disputed whether the civil courts should have a *locus*.[8]

1.3   Courts of the Church of Scotland

1.3.1   The General Assembly

The General Assembly meets annually (currently in May) and lasts about a week. The voting membership of almost 800 is commissioned by all Presbyteries, and comprises equal numbers of ministers and elders, along with a much smaller number from the Diaconate.

The General Assembly is the legislating authority within the legal structure of the Church, passing Acts of the General Assembly, and Regulations, which are binding on the courts, members and office-bearers of the Church. These may most conveniently be found in the Extranet section of the Church's website, where they are brought up to date following each Assembly.[9]

The central administration of the Church is, in legal terms, the executive machinery of the General Assembly; and so much of the business of the Assembly consists of receiving from Councils and Committees written Reports of their diligence and policy suggestions.

To complete the traditional elements of a legal system, the General Assembly is the final appeal court, able to receive appeals against the decisions of Presbyteries (both in their first-instance and appellate roles), and petitions seeking review of the decisions of executive bodies. Section 1.5 below, and Chapter 2, discuss the appeal processes of the Church, most of which are not now exercised directly by the General Assembly itself.

The General Assembly has an extensive set of Standing Orders, which remain substantially identical from year to year, but may

---

[8] Most recently the following case tested the boundary of jurisdictions in respect of the employment rights of non-inducted ministers: *Percy (AP) (Appellant) v Church of Scotland Board of National Mission (Respondent) (Scotland)* [2005] UKHL 73; 2006 SC (HL) 1. The substantive issue here has been resolved in a radical way by the Church, which has recently adopted the practice of employing (in the full, secular sense of the term) all its working ministers except inducted parish ministers.
[9] http://www.churchofscotlandextranet.org.uk/xchurchlaw/xchurchlawindex.htm.

be altered by the General Assembly to take account of changes of practice, or corrected by the Clerks to take account of minor developments (eg changes to the constitution of a Committee). The Standing Orders govern questions of membership, debate and judicial process, as well as the shape of executive bodies and the rules to determine their membership.

1.3.2   The Synod

Synods were large regional bodies, which latterly had few powers and responsibilities. They were abolished in 1992, and are mentioned here because it may be important to be aware of them when undertaking any research on a particular question.

1.3.3   The Presbytery

The Presbytery, despite its name, was the last of the Church's courts to emerge after the Reformation. It began as a place of spiritual exercise (Bible study, prayer and so on) but gradually evolved into a court like the others, covering a smaller region than the Synod. It might be said to be the "characteristic" court in the system, because it is a court of first instance for many purposes, but it can hear appeals against the decisions of Kirk Sessions, while its own decisions may be appealed to the General Assembly or its Commissions. This multi-dimensional nature of the Presbytery probably makes it the most useful and interesting to study.

The most solemn executive function of the Presbytery is the superintendence of the congregations, Kirk Sessions, ministers and deacons within its bounds. Superintendence of congregations is exercised regularly, normally on a 5-year cycle. Non-routine interventions may, and indeed should, be made whenever the Presbytery becomes aware of circumstances suggesting that there is a situation requiring its attention. The most serious of these interventions, in cases where a disciplinary offence has been alleged, are described in Chapter 4.

The most solemn ceremonial functions of the Presbytery are the ordination of ministers and deacons, the induction of parish ministers, and the formal introduction of other members of ministry teams. These symbolic acts of Presbytery helpfully remind the Church of the ongoing responsibility of superintendence exercised by that court.

Presbyterianism is not a form of government by Presbytery, and neither is the General Assembly a federation or association of Presbyteries. Each court determines its own membership, and normally each court elects those who will serve on its committees. Most members of the General Assembly are commissioned by Presbyteries from among their ministers and deacons, and from the elders serving in the Kirk Sessions within their bounds; but the General Assembly scrutinises those commissions to ensure they are all in order. Likewise, Kirk Sessions commission elders to serve on the Presbytery in which they are located, but the Presbytery must scrutinise and agree to receive such commissions. Though the term "representative elder" is used of the person commissioned by the Kirk Session to the Presbytery, members of Presbyteries and the General Assembly should always make up their own minds on each debate and should not be mandated in advance by the court which commissioned them.

As for membership of committees, there was until recently quite an extensive system of appointment by Presbyteries of members of General Assembly committees. This is far less common now, and there is no such system operating between Kirk Sessions and Presbyteries, which determine their own committees' membership.

1.3.4   The Kirk Session

Each congregation is governed by its Kirk Session, the lowest in rank of the Church's courts. Moderated by the minister, and otherwise consisting of the ordained elders of the congregation, the Kirk Session always acts as a court of first instance, normally by receiving reports from its Committees or office-bearers. It is extremely rare, though entirely possible, for a Kirk Session to receive an Overture or a Petition. The likelihood of lawyers appearing before Kirk Session meetings these days is very small because the discipline over parishioners is no longer the very formal moral exercise it once was.

It may be useful to note that ministers are subject to the Presbytery, and never to the Kirk Session, in all matters relating to life, doctrine and the exercise of ministry. It is neither legally competent nor pastorally appropriate for a Kirk Session to discuss these matters, and any concerns in this area should simply be conveyed to the Presbytery.

1.4   Officials of the Courts of the Church

1.4.1   Moderator

Each court is chaired by a Moderator. In the case of the Kirk Session, the permanent Moderator is the inducted minister of the charge, or the Presbytery-appointed Interim Moderator in times of vacancy or long-term absence of the minister. The minister and Kirk Session may arrange for particular meetings to be chaired by another member of the Session, but that individual has no moderatorial responsibilities or privileges between meetings.

The Presbytery elects a Moderator annually (the Presbytery year varies from place to place), and may choose any of its members, whether minister, elder or deacon. The Moderator presides at Presbytery services, with non-ministerial moderators deferring to a minister (eg his or her immediate predecessor) for the conduct of Communion services. Otherwise the Moderator provides impartial chairing of all the business of the Presbytery, and serves to some extent in a representative role on the court's behalf throughout his or her year in office. In a Presbyterian system, the Moderator has no further role of personal leadership, and should never be confused with a bishop: strictly, the equivalent of the bishop (ie the *locus* of *episkope*) is the Presbytery itself.

The Moderatorship of the General Assembly is, as befits the size and seniority of the court, a much more weighty office. Its holder may be a minister, elder or deacon, nominated by a committee of the General Assembly and formally appointed at the beginning of the Assembly week. The Moderator invariably takes a sabbatical of about 14 months from his or her normal duties, to prepare for the General Assembly and then to represent the Church nationally and internationally throughout the year of office. Again, there is no element of personal *episkope* in the role, and the Moderator has at most an ambassadorial role, including a calling to exercise prophetic leadership on behalf of the whole Church.

1.4.2 Clerk

Each court has a clerk, who is responsible for taking (and where necessary extracting) the minutes, keeping the papers and records of the court, handling correspondence and servicing the administrative needs of the court. Experienced clerks, in all courts, tend to acquire a role of advising on procedure, and holding the institutional memory of the organisation.

Session Clerks are usually members of the Kirk Session, but need not be, and their role is a voluntary and very part-time one. Presbytery Clerks are usually paid, and most exercise the role on a part-time basis; while the largest Presbyteries have full-time clerks, and some Presbyteries have permanent offices with support staff. The General Assembly has two clerks, based in the administrative offices in Edinburgh.

Anyone wishing to write to a court of the Church, to raise business with it, or to seek advice on questions of process, should approach the appropriate clerk in the first instance.

1.5   Types of Business at First Instance

1.5.1   Reports with Deliverances

In each court of the Church, the vast bulk of business consists of Reports brought by the executive bodies (which may be termed "Committees", "Councils", "Boards", "Working Parties" etc) responsible for implementing policy and developing new policy ideas. The Reports will demonstrate diligence in respect of previous instructions given by the court, and may suggest new initiatives, often in the form of proposals for fresh instruction by the court to the Committee.

Each Report has attached to it a Proposed Deliverance in numbered sections, being the motions the reporting body hopes the court will adopt. The first section is always a motion to "receive" the Report, and this is virtually always accepted without debate, except in the very unusual circumstance that there is felt to be something vexatious or incompetent about the Report as a whole. The court debates the Proposed Deliverance, discussing motions from the floor which may take the form of counter-motions and amendments. The resulting Final Deliverance provides the policy, instructions and resolutions of the court.

1.5.2   Overtures

An item of business may be brought on the initiative of one court to be considered by another, or may be brought to a court by some of its own members. The Overture takes substantially the same written form as a Committee's Report, and has a Proposed Deliverance attached, which is dealt with in the normal manner as above, though the court will normally place more significance on the decision whether to receive the Overture before considering the remainder of the Proposed Deliverance.

While many Overtures are brought by inferior courts to superior ones, the single most common use of Overture is to place before Presbyteries any proposal of the General Assembly to which the provisions of the Barrier Act of 1697 apply. This measure compels the General Assembly to consult the wider Church before innovating in the areas of worship, doctrine, discipline or church government, and the mechanism of an Overture is used whenever the Act is triggered by a particular piece of business.[10]

1.5.3 Petitions

Any individual or organisation, within or beyond the membership of the Church of Scotland, may petition any of its courts on any subject, provided a legitimate interest can be shown to justify doing so and the Petition passes the tests of competency and relevancy.

While the purposes for which Petitions are used are often similar to the purposes of Overtures, Petitioners do not enjoy the privilege afforded to the promoters of Overtures, ie they do not bring a Proposed Deliverance setting out exactly the terms of the remedy they seek. Instead, a Petition sets out a narrative, with the remedy sought set out in the form of a Crave. Upon consideration, it is up to the court to frame all the motions to be considered, which again may be subject to counter-motion and amendment.

Each of these types of business may produce an Appeal, or a Dissent and Complaint, providing of course that the General Assembly has not been the court of first instance.

1.6 Appeal; Dissent and Complaint

An Appeal may be taken by an individual or legal body against a decision of a Kirk Session or Presbytery, provided that the Appellant can demonstrate an interest in seeking the review of the original decision. The time-limit is very tight, and the clerk of the court appealed against should be contacted immediately.

A Dissent and Complaint may be taken by one or more members of the court appealed against. Apart from a slight difference in the rules about notice of intention to dissent and complain, the procedure is identical to that of Appeal. Indeed, the appealing parties in many cases comprise a mixture of members and non-members of the respondent court without any need to separate the complaint into separate cases.

For the avoidance of doubt, simple dissent may be entered against a decision to which objection is taken on a point of principle, without any element of complaint being taken to a superior court. Obviously, simple dissent is more commonly used in the General Assembly than elsewhere, since from the Assembly

---

[10] See J L Weatherhead (ed), *The Constitution and Laws of the Church of Scotland* (Edinburgh, 1997), p 153 for the text of the Barrier Act.

(as supreme court) there is of course no further resort and so no possibility of Appeal/Complaint.

The next chapter will describe the appellate bodies established in the Church of Scotland, each of which enables cases to be heard quickly, effectively and flexibly, rather than being heard (as once was the custom) by the whole General Assembly sitting as an appellate court. For civil lawyers, by far the most common engagement with the legal system of the Church of Scotland will take the form of appearance before one or another of these bodies.

Conclusion

This chapter has sketched the origins of the Presbyterian version of Christian polity; the current relationship of the Church of Scotland and the State; the courts of the Church; and the types of business transacted in those courts both at first instance and in their appellate functions.

CHAPTER 2

COMMISSIONS AND JUDICIAL BODIES

FINLAY A J MACDONALD

2.1 Introduction

The General Assembly has largely delegated its appellate judicial
function to two Commissions, namely the Commission of
Assembly and the Judicial Commission. In addition, a Ministries
Appeal Panel was established in 2007 for hearing certain classes
of appeal. This chapter will explain all three bodies in turn.
Meanwhile it is relevant to note that the one area in which the
General Assembly reserves to itself the right to hear appeals is
with regard to doctrine. "Heresy trials" are somewhat out of
fashion at the moment, though in the 1970s there were a number
of cases relating to "second baptism". These culminated in
an appeal heard by the 1976 General Assembly which upheld
a decision of a Presbytery (overturned by the Synod) that an
elder who had undergone second baptism had failed to fulfil his
ordination vows and could not continue in membership of the
Kirk Session.

Today, an issue which has the potential to result in judicial
proceedings on a matter of doctrine is human sexuality. In 2006
the General Assembly approved a proposal to authorise ministers
who were willing so to do to provide ceremonies to mark civil
partnerships. At the same time it was made clear that no minister
should be required to accede to requests for such ceremonies
contrary to conscience. The measure was referred to Presbyteries
under the Barrier Act, an Act of 1697 designed to prevent over-
hasty change and assist compliance with new law. However, the
measure failed to receive the approval of a majority of Presbyteries
and consequently fell. Since a failure to approve an enabling
measure falls well short of a decision to prohibit that which it was
intended to enable, the position now is that a minister providing
a service of blessing on a civil partnership could run the risk of a

disciplinary charge in his or her Presbytery. As such a case would turn on the interpretation and application of Scripture, it would inevitably come within the category of doctrine and, if appealed, the question would need to be determined by the General Assembly itself.

I turn now to the Commissions to which the General Assembly has delegated its appellate function in matters other than doctrine.

2.2 Commission of Assembly

"The practice of delegating to special commissioners the transaction of judicial and administrative business dates from the beginnings of the General Assembly's history."[1]

The one function not delegated is legislative.

2.2.1 History

Down to the 1980s, the Commission of Assembly met routinely for a day in October and February to deal with matters referred to it by the General Assembly which had met the previous May. The Commission's membership was co-terminous with that of the Assembly, plus one additional minister named by the Moderator. In effect, this additional person would chair the Commission in the probable absence of the Moderator on Church business. In practice, however, there was very little business for the Commission and in 1981 the General Assembly resolved that it should meet only when required. The result was that the Commission fell into abeyance until re-cast as a specific appellate body in 1997. This decision followed a review of the General Assembly itself, including a review of its appellate function.

One area which proved a fruitful source of Appeals and Dissents and Complaints was that of re-adjustment of congregations, now called "parish appraisal". Following the 1929 union between the Church of Scotland and the United Free Church, the united Church pursued a vigorous policy of rationalisation of ministerial and buildings resources. As ministers retired or moved, attempts were made to unite or link congregations. These were often resisted locally, resulting in Appeals which could be taken all the way to the General Assembly. In practice this meant late-night sittings while several hundred commissioners tried to get their heads round local geography, distances between communities

[1] J T Cox, *Practice and Procedure in the Church of Scotland* (Edinburgh, 6th edn, 1976), p 201.

and even the effects of tides upon island-linking causeways. The prevailing view was that there had to be a more efficient way of dealing with such matters!

The solution was to reorganise the Commission of Assembly into a much smaller body comprising one-tenth of the membership of the General Assembly which appointed it and to give it specific powers to hear and dispose finally of Appeals and Dissents and Complaints other than those which fell to be dealt with by the Judicial Commission or Ministries Appeal Panel. We will come to these in due course.[2] For completeness it should be noted that the Commission retains a general power to act on behalf of the Assembly other than in the field of legislation but, in practice, it now works largely as an appellate body, mainly, but not exclusively, in the area of parish appraisal.

2.2.2 Process

The Moderator of the General Assembly presides at meetings of the Commission, failing which the Commission has the power to appoint one of its own number to moderate. The Clerks of Assembly act as clerks to the Commission and the Procurator and Solicitor of the Church are also in attendance.

When an Appeal or Dissent and Complaint falling within the Commission's jurisdiction is received by the Clerks of Assembly the first thing to be considered is the question of competency. This is done by a Committee on Overtures and Cases which comprises the Clerks of Assembly, the Procurator (the Church's standing counsel) and the Solicitor of the Church. Where the Committee takes the view that the Appeal is not competent, and the Appellant wishes to persist in face of this advice, the Commission will first be asked to determine this question, with the appellant being given the opportunity to argue against the committee's opinion. Where the matter is clearly competent, the Assembly Clerks will immediately proceed to seek answers from the Presbytery as Respondent. They will also, through the Legal Questions Committee, appoint an Investigating Committee to prepare an agreed statement of facts in the case. This has proved an extremely helpful provision in reducing questions of fact and enabling members of the Commission to concentrate on arguments relating to the merits of the case and questions of law. There is no

---

[2] The legislation setting out the powers and functions of the Commission of Assembly as currently constituted can be found in General Assembly Act VI 1997.

provision for the calling of witnesses, though the convener of the Investigating Committee is in attendance and may be questioned by any member of the Commission. The Commission proceeds on the basis of statements by the parties, with the Appellants arguing their case and the Respondents replying. The Appellants are given an opportunity to make a further statement, particularly with regard to any new matter introduced by the Respondents. Thereafter the Respondents may make further reply. Parties may, if they choose, be represented by a solicitor. Following the party pleadings, members of the Commission may ask questions of either party. Parties themselves may not ask questions of each other. Once questions are exhausted parties are technically removed (normally remaining in their places) and the Moderator calls for motions. These must relate to the granting or dismissal of the Appeal, either *simpliciter* or to a specified extent. Debate between or among motions may then ensue. Before a vote is taken the Clerk reminds commissioners that only those who have heard all the pleadings at the bar may vote and that their judgment must be based solely on the pleadings.

The judgment of the Commission is final and, indeed, the legislation expressly declares that the General Assembly shall not hear or dispose of cases which fall within the Commission's jurisdiction; neither shall the Assembly review the Commission's judgments. However, where, in the opinion of the Commission, an important issue of principle is at stake this may be referred to the General Assembly. In the 11 years during which the Commission has operated in this way, no such reference has been made.

2.2.3 Powers

Mindful of the Church's independent jurisdiction as recognised in the Church of Scotland Act 1921 and the Articles Declaratory appended thereto, the legislation delegating powers to the Commission declares:

> "The following powers are hereby delegated to the Commission, and this delegation to the Commission constituted in accordance with this Act is declared to be consistent with the law and practice of the Church hitherto and in accordance with the Articles Declaratory of the Constitution of the Church in Matters Spiritual as hereby interpreted by the Church."

It has also recognised that the principle of *delegatus non potest delegare* applies and that it is not open to the Commission to remit the determination of the case to a small Special Commission, something which the General Assembly itself had done on occasions prior to 1997.

2.3 The Judicial Commission

2.3.1 History

In 1935, following the 1929 union, the General Assembly had enacted new legislation setting out the procedures to be followed in cases of discipline. Two years later, a report to the General Assembly proposed the setting up of a Judicial Commission "with a view to securing the more satisfactory disposal of causes coming up by way of Appeal from the Inferior Courts of the Church, and more particularly of cases affecting character and conduct". This proposal was referred to Presbyteries and finally agreed by the General Assembly of 1940. The new Judicial Commission had a membership of 48 ministers and elders. It was not given complete finality of judgment, to the extent that its findings had to be reported to the General Assembly, with the Assembly required to indicate approval or otherwise to these. Assembly members could ask questions of the Chairman of the Commission but, when it came to indicating acceptance or non-acceptance of the findings, this was to be done without debate. Thereafter the Appellant could enter a plea of mitigation before any censure was imposed. In the event that the findings of the Judicial Commission were not accepted, the Assembly itself then had to decide how to proceed.

2.3.2 Act I 1988

The role of the Judicial Commission was to hear Appeals arising out of disciplinary proceedings affecting ministers and probationers. However, in 1954 the General Assembly introduced new legislation in the form of an Act anent Congregations in an Unsatisfactory State. This allowed a Presbytery to dissolve the pastoral tie (remove a minister from his charge), or remove an office-bearer from office or a member from the congregation, if the unsatisfactory state was held to be "due wholly or substantially to defects or errors personal to the minister" or "due wholly or partly to the fault of any office-bearers or members specified". The Act provided that such a judgment could be "subject to appeal or complaint in ordinary form to the Superior Courts", namely Synod and General Assembly. However, by revised versions of both the 1940 and 1954 Acts, the General Assembly of 1960 determined that Appeals under the Unsatisfactory State legislation, where fault was attributed to an individual, should be heard by the Judicial Commission.

The 1960 legislation was further revised in 1988, with two new Acts that year anent Congregations in an Unsatisfactory State and a Judicial Commission. With regard to the former, the provision whereby an office-bearer or member could be removed was deleted, as were the references to defects and errors personal to the minister. These were replaced by a simple requirement that the Presbytery, after due inquiry in accordance with the provisions of the Act, should conclude "that the unsatisfactory state will continue unless the pastoral tie between minister and congregation is dissolved". Any Appeal by a minister so affected would continue to go to the Judicial Commission, but the Commission was now given full finality of judgment, the 1988 Act making it explicit that the findings and final judgment of the Judicial Commission would not be subject to review by the General Assembly. Both 1988 Acts remain current.

It should be noted that while dissolution of the pastoral tie is a catastrophic outcome for a minister, technically no fault is alleged and the removal of the minister from his or her charge is not to be understood as a disciplinary sanction. At the time of the 1988 amendments an analogy was made with the irretrievable breakdown of a marriage without attribution of fault to either party. The fact that the minister paid so high a price was seen simply as the only practical solution to an intractable problem. Such a minister remained in good standing and, indeed, provision was and continues to be made for financial support while he or she sought another charge.

While appeals arising from disciplinary proceedings affecting ministers, licentiates, graduate candidates for the ministry and deacons, and Appeals arising from the Unsatisfactory State legislation both come to the Judicial Commission, the two processes are dealt with quite differently at first instance.

A decision to dissolve the pastoral tie under Act I 1988 anent Congregations in an Unsatisfactory State is taken by a Presbytery following due process in accordance with the Act. The minister may then appeal to the Judicial Commission acting in the name of the General Assembly.

2.3.3   Act III 2001

While discipline of ministers also belongs to the Presbytery, and was directly administered by Presbyteries under the 1935 legislation referred to earlier, new legislation was brought in 2001 in the form of Act III of that year's General Assembly.

For the purposes of this discussion of appellate functions, when an Appeal is taken in an Act III case the parties before the Judicial Commission are the Appellant and the Committee of Presbytery that originally investigated the case. The Presbyterial Commission, whose judgment is being appealed, provides a Report in writing on the case generally and in particular on the grounds of appeal contained in the Note of Appeal.

2.3.4   Process

The membership of the Judicial Commission comprises 48 ministers and elders, including a Chairman and Vice-Chairman, appointed by the General Assembly. The *quorum* is 16 and at least 24 members must be present before a hearing can begin. Only those present throughout the whole proceedings may vote. The Appellant may object to any member of the Commission acting in the case and it is for the other members of the commission to sustain or repel such objection. The findings and final judgment of the Judicial Commission are reported in writing to the General Assembly, but simply for information and record purposes. Within 14 days of the hearing of an appeal the Commission produces written reasons for its findings.

The Clerks of Assembly act as Clerks to the Commission. Neither the Procurator nor Solicitor takes part in the proceedings.

As with the Commission of Assembly, the legislation (General Assembly Act II 1988) expressly declares that the delegation of power by the General Assembly to the Judicial Commission is in accordance with the *Articles Declaratory of the Constitution of the Church in Matters Spiritual.*

2.4   Ministries Appeal Panel

The General Assembly of 2007 established an Appeals Panel with powers to hear and dispose finally of appeals by individuals against decisions of the Ministries Council or any of its Committees relating to questions of recruitment, selection, education and training for the full-time Ministry of Word and Sacrament, the Auxiliary Ministry, the Diaconate and the Readership. Previously, such appeals were considered by the Commission of Assembly.

The Panel comprises a Convener, Vice-Convener and three members all appointed by the General Assembly. At least one must be legally qualified, one must be a minister and one an elder. The quorum is three, including either the Convener or Vice-Convener and including at least one minister and one elder (each of whom may be the Convener or Vice-Convener). The Principal Clerk, whom failing the Depute Clerk, acts as Secretary to the Panel.

2.5   Special Commissions

From time to time the General Assembly appoints Special Commissions, effectively *ad hoc* Committees, to address specific questions. In certain cases Commissions have been given finality of judgment; in others they have been required to report back with recommendations. Such Commissions may have a quasi-judicial role but an indication of the range of matters referred to Special Commissions can be judged from some recent examples:

- investigation of grievances raised by staff of particular central departments;
- review of particular policy decisions made by central Committees;
- re-examination of the primary purposes of the Church and formulation of proposals for continuing reform;
- assessment of the effect of organisational changes on the constitutional basis of the Church;
- review of the Church's role as a national Church with a commitment to a territorial ministry.

The General Assembly appoints the members of Special Commissions through the Selection Committee, a body appointed by every General Assembly to be available to consider names in the event of a proposal to appoint a Special Commission for some particular purpose.

The General Assembly of 2000 resolved that the Assembly was not an appropriate forum for the discussion of individual grievances which should be addressed through normal employment channels. It is therefore unlikely that individual cases would be referred to a Special Commission.

CHAPTER 3

PROCEDURE IN CHURCH COURTS

MARJORY A MacLEAN AND LAURA J DUNLOP

3.1 Introduction

The latter part of this chapter will discuss the sorts of contentious causes in which legal agents or representatives are most likely to be involved. This first section deals with more general procedure in the courts and Commissions of the Church.

Several types of distinction are used to classify types of business, but all have limitations. One obvious way of categorising business is as "legislative", "executive" and "judicial". This causes slight difficulty, because Overtures and Petitions are normally referred to generally as "cases", suggesting that they belong to the judicial category. However, some Petitions and the majority of Overtures relate to matters which might have been raised as straightforward legislative or executive business and without recourse to these special and relatively unusual instruments; and often they are non-contentious.

Another distinction between types of business, then, is that of "contentious" and "non-contentious" business. The General Assembly's Standing Orders[1] provide that, in a "contentious case", only those who have heard the whole oral pleadings may vote. One problem here is that the difficulty above with the definition of "case" is not resolved. Another is that it is possible to infer from the Standing Order that only "cases" can be contentious; whereas a great deal of hotly contended business is transacted by each of the courts of the Church acting in its routine work. The word "contentious" is perhaps better rendered "contested" in a judicial context, to avoid confusion.

Therefore it is equally unsatisfactory to classify business according to whether it originates in a Report, an Overture, a

---

[1] Standing Order 72 – see Appendix.

Petition, a process regulated by an Act (eg the disciplinary process described in Chapter 4) or an Appeal or Dissent and Complaint. The last of these are, by definition, contentious/contested, but all the others may vary.

In the second part of this chapter, therefore, several aspects of procedure in contested causes are examined, and may be used in different sorts of case. First, the kinds of business which do not involve parties formally opposed to each other are more briefly treated.

3.2   Procedure: Non-contested Business

3.2.1   Reports: the role of the reporting Convener

Most business in any court consists of receiving Reports and debating their Deliverances, as described in Chapter 1 above. The Convener of the reporting body may, but need not, be a member of the court, and is normally the only person taking part in the debate who is not doing so as an ordinary member of the court. There are no "parties" as such, and so it is never a formally contested form of process even if the substance of the debate may happen to be highly contentious and the discussion very heated.

As Standing Orders indicate, the Convener presents the Report, usually making a speech in support of a written Report already circulated to the court's voting members. Questions may be asked of the Convener at any time, by members of the court. At the end of any debate on a motion which is in any way at variance with the proposed Deliverance presented with the Report, the Convener has the right to close the debate before the vote is taken.

3.2.2   Order of debate

The Church of Scotland has a distinctive method for ordering debate. As will become apparent below, formal debate on motions does not normally involve those representing parties in cases, because it occurs after the formal "removal" of the parties from the process. However, it is described here so that parties questioning the quality of process in any case in an inferior court may judge whether there is procedural ground for appeal against this general standard of decision-making.

Broadly speaking, there are two types of motion which may be brought during the consideration of a proposed section of Deliverance: (1) a substantially alternative motion (referred to as a "counter-motion"); and (2) a motion adjusting any other motion (referred to as an "amendment" if it includes the removal of any words, and as an "addendum" if it consists only of the addition of words). Motions in the second category may seek to adjust the original motion, or any counter-motion, or any amendment or addendum itself not yet decided, whereas counter-motions can only be alternative to the original motion proposed.

Inevitably, in the course of complex debate, motions of every type may be raised in any order but the system copes with this unpredictability. Counter-motions are received and debated but voted on only after all motions have been received. All other motions are received and debated but each one is disposed of, for or against, before any other motion may be moved (with the necessary exception of the proposed amendment of a proposed amendment). By keeping to the rule that type (1) motions are never disposed of until all debate is exhausted, while type (2) motions are always disposed of immediately, the court minimises the number of proposals members must consider at once, while ensuring that the issues of most general principle (ie the broad alternatives) can be compared in their most perfected state.

When all debate is exhausted and all type (2) motions dealt with, the court then decides between/among the motion and counter-motion(s) to determine which is the motion before the court. The final step is for the prevailing motion (whether or not earlier amended) to be put simply for or against: this final step is necessary in any situation in which the *status quo* is a meaningful alternative for the court, but it is often omitted in situations in which the court is bound to make a positive decision of some kind (eg appeals), in which case anyone opposing the final motion must be presumed to have expressed that by supporting an (unsuccessful) counter-motion.

There are two major virtues of this system. First, no competent motion should ever have been closed off by earlier decisions because all options are kept open until the end of the debate. Second, there is never any need to move the direct negative of the original motion, as that (where it is meaningful) is provided for at the end of the voting process.

One other possibility is a motion to add a new section to a Proposed Deliverance without seeking to alter the existing sections. This is referred to as an addendum to the Deliverance (as opposed to an addendum to a section or to another motion); and it is vulnerable to counter-motions, amendments etc in the usual way.

In an Appeal, Dissent and Complaint or Petition, there are two differences from the description above. First, there is no original motion already before the court. When parties are technically removed and motions called for, the first motion is referred to as the "motion", and the second as the "(first) counter-motion", though both have come from the floor and they have equal status until disposed of by vote. Second, there is usually no reporting Convener, and therefore no speech formally closing any debate.

3.2.3   Enacting legislation

Only the General Assembly has a legislative function. It exercises this in the course of routine debates on Reports, as follows. The proposed Act or Regulation is set out in the Report (often as an Appendix), and a section of the proposed Deliverance invites the General Assembly to enact the measure. Where the proposal is subject to the provisions of the Barrier Act (described in Chapter 1) the process of sending Overtures to Presbyteries forms the substance of the section of the Deliverance. There is no difference in process between legislative and routine administrative business in the General Assembly, and no extra step in the scrutiny of proposed legislation.

There is no clear definition that assists reporting bodies to know when to propose an Act, a Regulation or a simple Deliverance to achieve their purpose. As the supreme court of the Church, the Assembly expects those subject to its jurisdiction to obey all its instructions, and so to some extent these forms of decision have equal authority. In recent practice, Acts have tended to be used to introduce new substantive rules which the Church wishes to be promulgated universally through its structures and to be easily referenced and very easily found, indefinitely, until repealed. Regulations have been used to indicate procedural methods to be used, and are often addressed to more defined bodies or officials. Deciding on the correct form is often more art than science.

3.2.4   Overtures and Petitions

The bringer of an Overture addresses the court in support of the written Overture, observing any time-limits contained in the Standing Orders of that court. He or she may be required to answer questions from members of the court, as these are in order to anyone and at any time. If a member of the court moves that an Overture be received, he or she has the ordinary rights of membership thereafter (including the right to vote), but has no other particular role in the debate.

The court is entitled to classify an Overture as belonging naturally within the debate on the report of a particular reporting body, and to treat the Proposed Deliverance of the Overture as a proposed new section of Deliverance. This has the single procedural effect that the reporting Convener has a right of reply to the debate.

A petitioner addresses the court in support of the written Petition, and answers questions as above. Before debate is called for, he or she is technically removed from the bar of the court, and recalled only for the formal intimation of the outcome.

Again, the court may wish to take the Petition in the course of a relevant debate. Since the starting point does not involve an original motion, the usual formula utilised is for the court to agree "to treat any motion to grant the crave of the Petition as a proposed addendum to the Deliverance".

3.2.5   References

A little-used mechanism is that of formal Reference, in which a court of first instance, believing itself to be incapable of making a competent or impartial or otherwise adequate decision on any kind of matter, may transmit it to the next superior court for disposal. The superior court first decides whether to accept the Reference, which it is not obliged to do if it believes the lower court ought to be able to deal with it; and if it receives the Reference only then does it turn to the substantive issue and dispose of it.

3.3   Procedure: Contested Cases

3.3.1   Adversarial and inquisitorial elements

The very long history of the Church of Scotland as a legal system has produced a hybrid system of dispute resolution: part adversarial and part inquisitorial. Cases are heard and decided using four elements:

(1) written pleadings, with Answers but no process of Adjustment;

(2) oral pleadings, with opportunity for response to new material, continuing back and forth at the discretion of the Moderator;

(3) questions put by members of the court or Commission to either party; and

(4) debate (as already described) from which the parties are excluded by technical removal from the proceedings.

3.3.2   *Determination of fact*

Questions of fact are decided in different ways, according to the particular type of case being heard. Each type of case is regulated by an Act of the General Assembly, which contains its own rules of procedure. For example, Act I 1988 anent Congregations in an Unsatisfactory State provides for an investigating committee to be established by the Presbytery, and it is given strong powers to pursue an inquisitorial process, producing an authoritative report upon the basis of which the Presbytery makes the decisions required by the Act. By contrast, Act III 2001 anent the Discipline of Ministers (and others) provides similarly for an investigating Committee to be set up, this time with such inclusive powers that the Presbytery retains no right of direction over it until the case is completed. Here, however, the case (including the determination of fact) is decided by a separate body, the Presbyterial Commission, so the Presbytery's Committee is committed to an adversarial fact-finding process. (For more on the Act III process, see Chapter 4 below.)

Almost all Appeals or Dissents and Complaints not governed by any other Act will fall to be heard by the Commission of Assembly, and be regulated by Act VI 1997. Here, the investigating committee is serving the appellate body, having the authority of its parent body to make a full and final determination of fact, based on an inquisitorial process of interview, examination of evidence etc. The committee publishes its findings in fact in the form of a written Report, which is circulated with the written pleadings to the members of the Commission of Assembly. The Convener of the investigating Committee appears before the Commission as it hears the case, and may be asked questions by members, though not by parties.

In the unusual event of a case (eg one involving doctrine) being felt by the Commission to be beyond its competence, the General Assembly would probably be guided by its Committee on Overtures and Cases to determine how evidence would be presented and facts determined by the whole Assembly.

3.3.3

In proceedings before a Church court or Commission which makes its own findings of fact, the rules of civil evidence in Scots law apply.[2] As is usual in secular courts, the burden of proof of any allegations made will lie on the party initiating proceedings. The standard to which the allegations must be proved is the balance of probabilities.[3] In applying this standard, courts take into account that the more improbable an allegation, the heavier will be the weight of evidence required to establish it. Other aspects of the hearing are described below but legal advice should be sought by any individual facing a contested hearing before a Church court or Commission, and reference should be made to standard Scots law textbooks on evidence for greater detail.

Before the hearing

In contested proceedings within the Church, it is likely that the court or Commission will make an order for the lodging of lists of witnesses and productions in advance of the hearing.[4] If difficulty is encountered in securing the attendance of a witness, there is authority for the proposition that Church courts may invoke the assistance of the sheriff court.[5]

Natural justice; human rights

The courts and Commissions of the Church will observe the principles of natural justice in their proceedings. This involves allowing sufficient time and opportunity for each party to prepare and then present his or her case, and guarding against any possibility of bias. If there is any reason of personal or pecuniary interest why an individual should not be involved in hearing a case, it is his or her duty to decline to act, and objection may be taken if he or she does not. As justice must be seen to be done, both the actuality and the appearance of a process are important. The test is whether the fair-minded and informed observer, having considered the facts, would conclude that there was a real possibility of bias.[6] Where Article 6 of the European Convention on Human Rights offers protection additional to that available under domestic law, for example the right to a public hearing, the courts and Commissions of the Church will offer the same rights.

---

[2] See, for example, Act III 2001, s 14(1).
[3] *Ibid.*
[4] Provision is made for this in proceedings under Act III 2001 – see s 11(8).
[5] *Lewis Presbytery* v *Fraser* (1874) 1 R 888.
[6] *Porter* v *Magill* [2002] 2 AC 357.

Witnesses

There are very few limitations on who can be a witness, but not every one who can be called can be made to testify. Privilege, in the sense of the right to refuse to answer a question, may apply. Anyone can refuse to answer a question if the answer could lead to his or her conviction for a criminal offence. Communications between a husband and wife during the subsistence of their marriage are privileged, as are communications between a legal adviser and his client. Other relationships described in ordinary parlance as "confidential", such as doctor and patient, are not so regarded in court unless, perhaps, the upholding of confidentiality would not prejudice the interests of justice. A child may be a competent witness but, in relation to the giving of evidence by those under 16 and other vulnerable witnesses, legislation exists for their protection and regard must be had to its terms. It is bad practice to have witnesses in court listening to evidence before they testify, and permission should always be sought from the court in advance if, for some reason, this is thought necessary. This does not apply to a party, who is entitled to remain throughout, or to an expert witness who may require to hear the evidence of fact before giving an opinion. It is also competent to call the opposing party as a witness.

At the hearing

Evidence may be oral, real or documentary. Oral evidence is the testimony of witnesses, who will be asked to take the oath or affirm. Real evidence is physical – the state of an object, or a place. If necessary, a visit may be made to a place the features of which are important to a case but this is unusual and photographs normally suffice. Documents should be agreed between the parties – an agreement that documents are what they bear to be is usually enough. Sometimes, however, a witness may be needed to "speak to" (ie explain) a particular document which is controversial – perhaps a handwritten letter, for example. In these circumstances, the best evidence is always that of the writer. Alternatively, if a document is uncontroversial, it may be agreed as the evidence of its author, thereby superseding the need to call him or her as a witness. If these steps are taken, this is usually recorded in an agreement between the parties known as a Joint Minute, which is presented to the court at the start of proceedings. Other facts agreed between the parties can also be set out in such a Minute.

Evidence is led from the party bearing the burden of proof and then, if he or she wishes, from the other party. The manner of leading evidence will be as in a secular court: evidence in chief is led by the party calling the witness, followed by cross-examination and, if so advised, re-examination by the first questioner. Witnesses may refresh their memory from notes, provided that the notes were made at the time of the event in issue. Objection may be taken to individual questions, for example on the basis of relevancy or lack of fair notice. Leading questions should be confined to cross-examination, unless the matters to be elicited are uncontroversial. An objection may be upheld, repelled or reserved. Reserving an objection means allowing the question subject to questions of competency and relevancy being argued during submissions at the end of proceedings.

Following submissions, the court will reach its decision. In so doing, it will consider the credibility and reliability of witnesses. The former refers to truthfulness, the latter to clarity of recall. These matters should only be judged on the whole evidence as, plainly, a witness whose evidence appears credible and reliable when given may be contradicted by a later witness. The court should reach its conclusions only on the basis of the evidence led before it, although certain matters are within judicial knowledge and do not require to be proved. Examples of these could be matters of geography or history, current affairs, basic science, the calendar and so on.

3.3.4   Entitlement to representation and costs

The right to be represented before a court, and the right to have that representation paid for from the funds of the Church, are different considerations.

The Church's practice in the matter of legal representation in its courts may be summarised by the following principle: there is no right to legal representation where no pecuniary interest is at stake. So, for example, the Kirk Session exercises no judicial authority over anyone with a financial interest in its decisions, and any prejudicial decisions they do make would be administrative ones which could be challenged in civil law; so there has never been a right of legal representation before the Session. On the other hand, and demonstrating the obverse of this principle, cases heard by the Judicial Commission (Act II 1988) always have the capacity to affect the patrimonial interests of a minister or other Respondent, and the Act particularly provides that the right to representation cannot be qualified.

The right to have legal advice or representation paid for by the Church is mainly regulated by the legislation governing each sort of process. The most extensive scheme is contained in Act III 2001 anent Discipline of Ministers (and others), which is the subject of Chapter 4. It is another illustration of the "patrimonial interest" rule of thumb that Act IV 2007 anent Bullying, for example, specifically provides that the funds of the Church shall never be available for this purpose, because those who are subject to the discipline of that Act, and the censures available in it, are such that no patrimonial or professional interest is at stake.

In any case where the answer to either of these questions is not clearly determined in the relevant Act of the General Assembly, parties would normally contact the Clerks of the Assembly who would take advice from the Committee on Overtures and Cases or, if necessary, the Legal Questions Committee of the General Assembly.

3.4   General Procedure

Lawyers appearing in the courts and Commissions of the Church often find it helpful to know the particular practices and courtesies they should be expected to follow. A very few general tips may be worth bearing in mind.

Any meeting of a court or Commission is constituted by an opening prayer (which may be amplified to become a more extended act of worship) and closed also with prayer (often in the form of the pronouncing of the Benediction). It is strongly recommended that parties and representatives appearing in the first case of any meeting should be present for the opening, regardless of their personal religious beliefs. If followed by other business, it is in order to withdraw when one's one case is completed. In the same spirit, parties and representatives arriving during the meeting to take part in the last item of business should remain until the meeting has been closed or adjourned.

Representatives appearing before Presbyteries, the General Assembly, or any Commission, should bring their bar gown and in most circumstances will find it is appropriate to wear it. Counsel appearing in appellate cases, or before the General Assembly in Petitions, should wear wigs. The practice of bowing to the Moderator should be observed as to the Bench in a civil court, and will normally be observed by members of the court in the same manner.

All remarks should be addressed to the Moderator, and the court should be addressed by the term "Moderator". In oral pleadings the first and very last sentence should begin "Moderator", which is better not used otherwise as it is often interpreted as a signal for the Moderator to stand. In answering questions, there is no need to use the word "Moderator", as long as it is generally borne in mind that the court is being addressed through its chair.

The most general, and obvious, comment to make is that representatives should bear in mind two characteristics of the court's members. First, many are not legally qualified and should be addressed so far as possible in terms comprehensible to legal laymen even when matters of law are being debated. Second, the court operates within the Church's spiritual jurisdiction: this has implications for the criteria upon which decisions will be made, and also, of course, upon expectations of conduct, language used, and so on.

It is perfectly in order to consult the Clerk of the Court or Commission in advance to clarify all questions of process or conduct. It is well understood that lawyers normally have little experience within this special jurisdiction, and those appearing for the first time will find they are treated with generosity and forbearance.

CHAPTER 4

THE PRESBYTERIAL COMMISSION:
LAW AND PRACTICE

JANETTE S WILSON

4.1 Introduction

Discipline is one of the areas falling within the Church's separate
spiritual jurisdiction in matters spiritual. Those who may be
disciplined in the courts of the Church are those who hold office
in the church, communicant members and adherents. No appeal
lies beyond the Church to civil courts or employment tribunals
although cases such as *Logan* v *Presbytery of Dumbarton*[1] which
was heard in the Court of Session recognised limited grounds
where judicial review might be competent – for example, for
exceeding jurisdiction.

The civil courts will aid the Church courts to cite witnesses
to attend – see the sheriff court case of *Presbytery of Lewis* v
Fraser.[2] This is a practical example of Article VI of the Declaratory
Articles which refers to the mutual duties which the Church and
the State owe to each other.

This chapter, however, deals only with the discipline of
ministers and other ordained persons.

4.2 The Historical Perspective

Before 2001, the process by which a disciplinary offence against
a minister or probationer was dealt with was known as a trial
by libel, the libel being a statement of the alleged offence. The
whole process was, from beginning to end, carried through by
the Presbytery to which the minister was answerable for matters
of life and doctrine. The then procedures were based on Assembly
legislation dating from 1707 which had not changed greatly over

---

[1] *Logan* v *Presbytery of Dumbarton* 1995 SLT 1228.
[2] *Presbytery of Lewis* v *Fraser* (1874) 1 R 888.

the years although latterly they were set out in Act VII 1935 and, to a lesser extent, in Act XIX 1889. The Basis and Plan of Union between the United Free Church and the Church of Scotland of 1929 in the section on discipline stated "it is the right of the courts of the Church to adjudicate in all matters of discipline and the courts should not be both prosecutor and judge".

However, a number of provisions in the 1935 Act potentially allowed a Presbytery to depart from this. For example, it required the Presbytery to prepare the libel and gave it the option of prosecuting with the evidence being heard by a committee of its own number with or without external Assessors. The Presbytery acting as prosecutor and judge and jury clearly was neither compatible with natural justice nor compliant with Human Rights legislation. The language of the 1935 Act with its reference to libels and *fama* (a scandalous report) and *fama clamosa* (public scandals) was not helpful. 1997 saw the small Presbytery of Angus in the case involving Miss Helen Percy endeavouring to operate the somewhat archaic procedures in the spotlight of huge media attention. This exposed very clearly the deficiencies of the Act and urgent steps were put in hand to discuss reform. After careful deliberation, it was concluded that the best course was first to leave with the Presbytery concerned the task of investigating and prosecuting the case but doing so via a small Committee with minimal involvement of the whole Presbytery. Second, a new body should be set up which would be completely independent of the Presbytery and would hear the case, rule on it and, where wrongdoing was established, impose an appropriate censure. With considerable assistance from the then Procurator, Alastair Dunlop, QC, an Act replacing the previous legislation was presented to the 2000 Assembly. Removing as it did the judging of the case from the jurisdiction of the Presbytery (albeit leaving it with the right to appoint the Committee with the Investigatory and prosecuting role), the Act's provisions were innovative and required Barrier Act procedure. The Act therefore came into force in 2001 as Act III 2001.[3]

4.3   The 2001 Act

The Act in its title sets out those to whom it applies, ie ministers and those on their way to become ministers and also Deacons who work full time in parishes assisting ministers. For

---

[3] The 2001 Act can be viewed at: http://www.churchofscotland.org.uk/extranet/xchurchlaw/xchurchlawacts.htm.

convenience, such persons will all be referred to as "ministers" or as the "Respondent" (which is the terminology in the 2001 Act).

The 2001 Act has been amended every year since passed. This does not mean that it was badly drafted – experience has shown this not to be the case. However, some changes have been made following feedback from both those representing the parties and those serving on the Commission. The Act has also had to reflect changing circumstances – for example, provisions required to be introduced in the light of the Protection of Children (Scotland) Act 2003 ("POCSA") and the introduction of enhanced disclosure checks for ministers.

In the same way as the Act required Barrier Act procedure, so do amendments which are other than minor.

4.4   The Investigatory Stage

Part 2 of the 2001 Act sets out in detail how the investigation is to be undertaken. A committee is to be set up when Presbytery receives notice that a disciplinary offence may have been committed by a minister. The conduct of the investigation is remitted to a Committee of three persons appointed by the Presbytery with at least one to be a minister and one an elder. They need not all be members of the Presbytery concerned. The technical definition of those persons over whom a particular Presbytery has jurisdiction is in s 2. The Act also provides for one Presbytery to refer a complaint on to the relevant Presbytery where it itself does not have jurisdiction – to cover, for example, cases where a disciplinary matter emerges after the minister has moved to another congregation.

The definition of what is a disciplinary offence is set out in s 1(1) as being:

> "Conduct which is declared censurable by the Word of God, Act of the General Assembly or established custom of the Church or a breach of a lawful order of any court of the Church."

In addition, s 3(3) and (4) set out three specific matters which are declared to be offences:

- speaking to the press (which applies both to the Respondent and any other member of Presbytery); and
- being placed on the Sex Offenders Register or the Disqualified from Working with Children list kept in connection with POCSA.

There was concern that the s 1 definition might prove difficult to construe, although it would clearly be impossible to have a list of all possible censurable conduct. In practice this has not been a difficulty so far. It is arguably no vaguer than, say, the test used by the Scottish Solicitors' Discipline Tribunal in cases involving solicitors which uses as a yardstick the concept of standards of conduct which competent and reputable solicitors would regard as serious and reprehensible. However, no case involving doctrine has so far been brought under the 2001 Act. That would no doubt involve a whole range of challenges.

The 2001 Act provides for a two-part procedure. First, the Committee appointed has to decide whether to investigate. There is effectively a "sift" to deal quickly with malicious complaints or where the conduct complained of, even if proved, would clearly not constitute a disciplinary offence. In these circumstances the Committee reports back to the Presbytery which can, however, issue instructions regarding the minister's future conduct.

However, if the Committee considers there is a case to answer, it gives notice to the Presbytery and the General Assembly's Legal Questions Committee which appoints a Legal Assessor who requires to be legally qualified. From that stage onwards both the Committee and the Respondent are entitled to be represented by counsel and/or a solicitor. (The matter of the payment of the costs of legal representation is dealt with later.) The two roles are separate. The Legal Assessor is there to advise in relation to procedures in terms of the Act but not to be directly involved in matters such as taking statements from witnesses and the like. The Assessor's position is a voluntary one, with Assessors being selected from a small pool.

The 2001 Act entitles the committee to carry out such investigations as it deems necessary so that it can determine whether a disciplinary offence may have been committed. At all stages, there are provisions designed to give fair notice of the allegations to the Respondent and to give the opportunity, if so advised, to answer these. If the Committee decides there is no *prima facie* case, it reports this conclusion back to Presbytery and any administrative suspension imposed is lifted.

Where the minister wishes to admit guilt at the investigatory stage, there is now an accelerated process which can be followed.

4.5 Administrative Suspension

The 2001 Act makes provision for a Respondent to be suspended administratively, with full payment of stipend continuing, at the initiation of the investigation or at any time this is deemed appropriate. This involves suspension from the duties of the Respondent's office, ie with his or her congregation and also from undertaking ministerial functions generally, such as conducting weddings outwith the parish. Since the 2001 Act was brought in, in all but one case, the Respondent has been suspended from the outset. In the one exception, the minister was suspended by the Presbytery after he admitted the charges in an amended notice of complaint.

If the Committee decide as a result of its investigations that there is a case, that leads to the next stage – the initiation of disciplinary proceedings.

4.6 Disciplinary Proceedings

The Committee has to draw up a notice of complaint which runs in name of the committee as the prosecuting body. This has to set out the alleged disciplinary offence or offences which the 2001 Act terms as "charges". The notice must specify the time and place of each charge and the facts necessary to constitute the disciplinary offence. In addition, a summary of the evidence which the committee considers supports each charge is also drawn up.

Care has to be taken with the notice of complaint, as it has to survive objections from the Respondent on grounds of competency and relevancy. The Presbyterial Commission can, however, agree to the notice being amended unless it sees just cause to the contrary (s 17). In a number of cases, objections have been taken to the wording of the notice.

The notice is then forwarded to the Solicitor of the Church (who acts as Secretary to the Commission) with a list of witnesses and proposed productions (but not, at that stage, the productions themselves). The Solicitor then proceeds to select the Commission to hear the case.

The 2001 Act provides for there to be a Convener and Vice-Convener and an alternate Convener and Vice-Convener, all to be qualified to practise as lawyers and appointed by the General Assembly. Initially the Vice-Conveners did not require to be legally qualified but early on it became apparent that this would be advisable and the 2001 Act was amended. Having alternates means that two cases can run simultaneously, which has happened. The practice has also developed of spreading the load by running the two Convener/Vice-Convener teams turn about as cases arise.

As well as the Convener and Vice-Convener, three persons, one at least to be a minister, are selected randomly from the Presbyterial Panel. As set out in s 1(e), each Presbytery is entitled to appoint one person in respect of every hundred members of Presbytery. The appointees require to be ministers, deacons or elders. The approach is to honour the traditional role of the Presbytery in determining such cases, although panel members cannot serve in any case involving their own Presbytery. Presbyteries are encouraged to appoint equal numbers of men and women. In fact, a large proportion of those put on the Panel by their Presbyteries, including the ministers, have some sort of legal background.

Once the Commission is selected, the Secretary of the Commission then issues an Order in name of the Commission appointing the date for the first diet and granting warrant for service of the notice of complaint. The Order contains a list of the names of those appointed to serve on the Commission – to forewarn the respondent in case any objection is to be taken to the Commission's composition.

The Committee then serves the order within the period fixed for this, along with the Notice of Complaint, the lists of witnesses and productions and the summary of evidence earlier prepared. This can be done by recorded delivery post or by sheriff officer and if need be a warrant for re-service can be granted.

Unless the Respondent admits to the charge or charges in the Notice of Complaint, the first diet is essentially a procedural hearing. The Act does allow for the first diet being dispensed with where there are no objections to the notice, the charges are denied and there are no other preliminary matters to be discussed. Challenges to the competency and relevancy of the complaint can be sustained or repelled or deferred until after proof. The Commission may permit the Notice of Complaint to be amended. Once any challenge has been dealt with, the Respondent has to state whether he or she admits or denies each of the charges which remain.

4.7 Procedural Motions

Such motions have in practice been on a variety of topics. In three cases, there have been motions that the proof should be taken in private. Section 12 of the 2001 Act provides for hearings to be in public except in very limited circumstances – such as that publicity would prejudice the private life of the parties or the interests of justice. The presumption in favour of justice not only being done but being seen to be done is strong and no s 12 motion has yet succeeded, whether coming from a Committee or a Respondent.

There have also been motions on such diverse topics as permitting a complainer to give evidence from behind a screen (refused), playing a probably illegally taped recording of a phone call (granted) and the obtaining of a psychiatric report on a respondent (a joint motion which was granted).

4.8 The Proof Hearing

Once such issues are disposed of and an estimate of the likely time needed provided by both sides, dates are then fixed for the proof. The Act requires that the proof should normally commence not less than 28 days nor more than 42 days after the first diet or any adjournment. The order fixing the proof will also contain a date by which the Respondent requires to intimate witnesses and productions and for the Committee to lodge any additional productions.

4.9 The Procedure at the Proof

The rules of Scots civil evidence apply, with the onus of proof being on the Committee. The standard of proof is on the balance of probabilities. The proceedings are recorded with the necessary arrangements for this being organised by the Commission. Witnesses take the oath or affirm. Regarding dress, lounge suits or equivalent are the order of the day with neither wigs nor robes being required. The Commission is addressed through the Convener.

A question arose in an early case about a witness who was reluctant to attend. The difficulty in fact resolved itself. For the avoidance of doubt, however, the General Assembly subsequently declared that the Commission had all the powers of a court of the Church, including the power of citation and the right to invoke the assistance of the sheriff court in compelling the attendance of witnesses. If, therefore, a problem is anticipated, a motion requires to be made to the Commission so that it can present the necessary application to the sheriff court.

At the hearing, the Committee first leads its evidence. The Committee's witnesses are first questioned by whoever is presenting the case for the Committee, then cross-examined by the Respondent or his or her legal representative, with the Committee's representative then being entitled to ask further questions in clarification of points already covered. The same procedure is followed with evidence being led by the Respondent's representative from the Respondent's witnesses and the Respondent, where he or she elects to give evidence followed by cross-examination and re-examination. Members of the Commission are also entitled to ask questions at any stage. Both sides' representatives then make submissions about the evidence led, with the Respondent having the right to speak last.

4.10   The Commission's Decision

This is either given on the day or subsequently at a later date. Decisions can be unanimous or by majority.

If the charge(s) are held to be established or are admitted, the Committee is heard in regard to an appropriate sentence and then the Respondent is heard in mitigation.

4.11   Censures

The Commission then has to decide as to which censure is to be imposed. The censures are set out s 1(1)(h) and are:

- *Reprimand*: an expression of disapproval of particular behaviour, with counsel regarding future conduct.
- *Suspension for a fixed period from the status and functions of ministry*: at the end of the period there is right of automatic restoration by the Presbytery on petition by the Respondent.
- *Suspension without limit of time*: the Commission is now required to state a minimum period of suspension. When that has expired, it is open to the Respondent to petition the Presbytery to request that the suspension be lifted. However, the Presbytery has absolute discretion whether to grant or refuse, subject to the usual right of appeal.
- *Removal of status*: the Respondent ceases to be a minister of the Church. However, although quite a high hurdle to get over, an application can be presented subsequently to the General Assembly's Ministries Council for restoration in terms of s 8 of Act IX 2002.

Suspension beyond a very short period will normally, and removal of status will always, result in the Presbytery severing the pastoral tie between the minister and his/her congregation. In other words, the congregation is declared vacant, an interim moderator is appointed and the congregation has to start looking for a new minister. The minister will be required to vacate the manse, although the Presbytery should allow a reasonable time for alternative accommodation to be arranged.

The Commission has to set out in writing its findings in fact, which charges it has found to be established, its reasons for imposing a particular censure and whether these decisions were unanimous or by majority. The Commission's judgments are public documents and are available from the Solicitor of the Church for those wishing to consult them.

4.12   Accelerated Process

It became clear that there was a need for an accelerated process to deal with cases where the minister is willing from the outset – or at least before the notice of complaint is served – to admit the conduct complained of and the Act was amended in 2008 by adding a new s 18A to allow for this. In such a case, the Respondent has to lodge with the Committee a written statement setting out all or which of the allegations he or she is willing to admit. Confirmation that the Respondent has received legal advice about the matter must be included. If the admission is acceptable to the Committee, either at once or after appropriate inquiries have been made, it arranges for a Joint Minute to be adjusted with the Respondent, setting out the offences admitted, a summary of the material facts and such information as may assist the Commission in reaching an appropriate disposal of the case. The Joint Minute is then sent to the Secretary of the Commission. A Commission is selected and a date for disposal of the case fixed. After hearing both sides, the Commission then proceeds to impose what it consider the appropriate censures and records this with reasons for the censure. Section 18A also provides that the Commission can take into account, as it sees fit, the early admission made to mitigate sentence.

4.13   Appeals

An Appeal lies to the Judicial Commission, unless on a matter of doctrine in which case the Appeal requires to go to the General Assembly. The Judicial Commission is described in Chapter 2 above, and Act II 1988 sets out its rules of procedure.

Appeal lies on both points of law and severity of censure. The latter is a relatively recent innovation. The two Appeals which have been taken were both arguably Appeals against the censure imposed which had been dressed up as being on points of law. Both were in fact refused but it was subsequently decided that there ought to be a right of appeal against sentence and the Act amended accordingly.

The Appeal requires to be lodged with the Clerks within 21 days of intimation of the Commission's written decision.

The parties to the Appeal are the Committee and the Respondent – which is unusual in church procedure. However, the Commission is entitled to lodge a Report commenting.

4.14   Expenses of Legal Representation

In recognition of the fact that legal aid is not available for procedures in the Church courts, up until 2007, all expenses as taxed by the Auditor of Court of Session were met with respect to the disciplinary proceedings out of central church funds. In addition, *ex gratia,* expenses relating to the investigatory stage were also met at least in part. Payment of expenses included automatically those relating to an Appeal (which meant that essentially there was no reason not to appeal and perhaps it says a lot for Respondents that only two appeals took place while this rule was in force). The expenses were "party–client third party paying". This led to a very heavy financial burden which was difficult to budget for and was a source of great concern to the General Treasurer of the Church.

Accordingly, the Act was amended. A reasonable measure of financial assistance is given but to a lesser extent than before. The same rules as to payment apply to representation for the Committee and for the Respondent.

The current arrangements are contained in s 22 and payment is made on a "party and party" basis only, with no percentage or other increases to apply.

Only the cost of a solicitor will be met unless the use of counsel is specifically sanctioned. Sanction can be applied for after the notice of complaint has been lodged and the Presbyterial Commission has been appointed to hear the case. The application is then submitted to the other Convener and Vice-Convener. There is a hearing. Parties are entitled to be present and make representations. If counsel is sanctioned, it is specified whether the sanction is for junior counsel only, for senior acting alone or for junior and senior and whether for the whole case or just part. "Junior counsel" is deemed also to refer to solicitor advocates. There are similar procedures in regard to representation at appeals. Decisions on these matters are not subject to appeal.

CHAPTER 5

SCOTTISH EPISCOPAL CHURCH: POLITY, LAW AND GOVERNANCE

A B WILKINSON

5.1 Introduction

This chapter is concerned with the fundamental principles of the law of the Scottish Episcopal Church and with the basis of its legal system in its polity and methods of governance, together with an outline of the Church's origins, character and institutional structure without which the legal system cannot properly be understood.

5.2 Origins and Historical Development

5.2.1 *Origins*

For nearly 130 years from the Reformation onwards, the governance and ecclesial character of the Church of Scotland fluctuated, often in circumstances of considerable conflict and ambiguity, between episcopacy and presbyterianism. The Scottish Episcopal Church emerges as a body distinct from the Church of Scotland only from the Revolution settlement of 1689. The Prelacy Act of that year abolished "Prelacy and all superiority of any office in the Church in this Kingdome above Presbyters" and the laws in favour of episcopacy which had prevailed since the Restoration were repealed. By subsequent legislation Episcopal clergy were to be ejected from their benefices[1] and the whole government of the church was put in the hands of the surviving Presbyterian ministers, about 60 in number, who had refused

---

[1] The process of ejection although energetically pursued was often delayed because of difficulty of enforcement and in 1695 an Act was passed which permitted Episcopal clergy to remain in their benefices if they took the oath of allegiance by 1 September of that year.

to accommodate to episcopacy at the Restoration and "such ministers and elders as they might admit and receive".

5.2.2   Post-Revolution history and organisation

The pre-Revolution Bishops, although devoid of recognition, office and authority in the eyes of the law, were careful to provide for succession to their order. Clergy loyal to Episcopalian principle remained and an interest in liturgical worship, which had been largely dormant during the Restoration Episcopate, began to revive. It is therefore possible to speak of an emergent Episcopal Church in the years following the Revolution but the times were confused and it took long for it to take an organised and definite shape. An inhibiting factor was the common view, with deep historical roots, that there could be no form of dissent from the established church. In 1709 the Rev James Greenshields opened a chapel in a private house in Edinburgh where he ministered to some members of the Church of England according to Anglican rites. He was prohibited by the Presbytery of Edinburgh from exercising the office of ministry on the grounds of "being within their bounds and without their allowance and introducing a form of worship contrary to the purity and uniformity of the church established by law". He refused to comply and, on application by the Presbytery, the magistrates of Edinburgh committed him to prison "there to remain until he should give security to desist from the exercise of the ministry within their bounds, or to remove himself from thence". An appeal to the Court of Session failed and the unfortunate Mr Greenshields languished in prison for some 7 months until eventually released on a successful appeal to the House of Lords. The case settled that the actings of Mr Greenshields were lawful but its consequences beyond that were uncertain. The law was clarified by the Scottish Episcopalians Act 1711 (commonly called the "Toleration Act") "to prevent the disturbing those of the Episcopal communion in Scotland in exercise of their religious worship" which gave Episcopalians the right, subject to certain conditions, to meet for worship and provided that there was to be "no civil pain or forfeiture or disability whatsoever" as a consequence of excommunication from the established church. The Act opened a path for development but that path was blocked by the Jacobite rebellions of 1715 and 1745 and the Jacobite sympathies of which Episcopalians were suspected. As a result penal laws were passed which subjected them to severe restrictions. "Qualified chapels" ministered to by clergy ordained in England and subject to English

Bishops were exempt from the penal laws but those chapels were separate from the Episcopal Church and the development of the indigenous church on an organised basis was presented with almost insuperable difficulties.

A first step towards reorganisation was taken in 1727 when the Bishops met in synod and passed six Canons mainly concerned with the election of Bishops by the presbyters (priests) of a diocese and the assigning of dioceses (or districts as they were then called out of deference to the supposed royal prerogative of assigning dioceses) to Bishops. That was followed in 1731 by articles of agreement among the Bishops relating to the election of a Primus or presiding Bishop, to the issuing of a mandate by the Primus for Episcopal elections and to the confirmation of Episcopal elections by a majority of Bishops. In 1743 a synod of Bishops passed 16 Canons affirming the articles of agreement of 1731, elaborating them in important respects and providing for a number of other matters concerned with church government. By 1743 the basic structures for the future government of the Church and its development seemed to be in place but then the 1745 rebellion intervened. The penal laws which followed were much more severe than those passed after 1715 and the Episcopal Church was reduced to a state in which it seemed likely to be extinguished.

The focus of concern about Jacobite loyalties was removed by the death of the Young Pretender in 1788 and in 1792 the penal laws were repealed although at the same time Episcopalian clergy were required under prescribed penalties and disabilities, to take the oaths of allegiance, abjuration and assurance, to pray at divine service for the Royal family and to subscribe the Thirty-nine Articles of Religion of the Church of England. The last requirement was a particular cause of offence which continued until the repeal of the Scottish Episcopalians Relief Act 1792 in 1977. It had, however, the advantage of facilitating relations with the Church of England and so with the wider Anglican Communion. It also opened the way to an accommodation with the qualified chapels and at a convocation held at Lawrencekirk in 1804 agreement was reached on terms on which qualified chapels might be accepted into the Episcopal Church.

5.2.3 Development of synodical government

In the 18th century, as has been seen, the election of a Bishop to a vacant see was, subject to approval by the College of Bishops, entrusted to the presbyters of the diocese and in 1863 laity were given a voice in the election of Bishops by lay electors chosen from each incumbency. In 1811 provision was made for a Provincial Council (subsequently styled a General or Provincial Synod) consisting of two houses, one of Bishops and the other of representative presbyters to whom was given power to negative any future legislation. Subsequent changes enlarged the representation of the clergy; from 1905 lay representatives were included in a consultative council on church legislation and in 1961 lay representation was introduced to the Provincial Synod. Along with those developments in legislative structures there had been a parallel development in the structures for oversight of administration, property and finance. In 1876 the Representative Church Council was set up, consisting of the Bishops and clergy, certain lay officials and a lay representative from every congregation, and recognised as the organ of the Church in matters of finance. In 1982 both the Provincial Synod and the Representative Church Council were abolished and their powers and functions merged in a new General Synod consisting of three houses, Bishops, clergy, and laity. That was a development which was paralleled about the same time in other provinces of the Anglican Communion and marked the recognition, which had always been present in the tradition but for long inadequately realised, of the part to be played by the whole people of God in the governance of the Church.

5.3   Ecclesial Character

5.3.1   *Reformed and Catholic*

As a body which emerges at the Revolution settlement from the Church of Scotland, the Scottish Episcopal Church has its roots in the Scottish Reformation. Those links with the Scottish Reformation make it unusual among churches of the Anglican Communion of which it forms part, most of which trace their origins, if indirectly, to the English Reformation. The Church, while recognising its inheritance from the Reformation, has sought to reconcile that with the maintenance of continuity with catholic tradition.[2] The emphasis on catholic continuity is reflected in the Episcopal character of the church and in the

---

[2] Emphasis has sometimes been put on the protestant inheritance particularly by those who associate themselves with the tradition of the qualified chapels which had tended to stress a protestant orientation often seen as in affinity with the English rather than the Scottish Reformation. In the aftermath of the reception of the qualified chapels the title "Protestant Episcopal Church in Scotland" was adopted in the heading of the Code of Canons of 1828 and retained despite controversy in 1829, only to be dropped in 1838.

opening words, commonly regarded as definitive, of the Code of Canons: "the Scottish Church, being a branch of the One Holy Catholic and Apostolic Church of Christ, retains inviolate in the sacred ministry the three orders of Bishops, Priests and Deacons, as of Divine Institution". It is also reflected in the liturgies and formularies of the Church and in the embodiment of its legislation in a Code of Canons.

5.3.2 Episcopate

In the Episcopal Church the Bishop is understood as representing in succession to the Apostles the focus of unity and authority within his diocese. That unity is seen, if in symbolic form, as a vertical unity with the historic tradition of the universal church from the earliest times and, if in necessarily impaired form, as a horizontal unity with the Bishops of the worldwide church. Each Bishop is regarded as belonging to the worldwide Episcopal College, expressing and serving the unity of the Church Catholic. Thus in the mandate issued by the Primus for the election of a bishop the electors are reminded that their choice "will necessarily affect the interests, not of your diocese only, but also of the Church throughout Scotland and of the Anglican Communion and of the Church Catholic throughout the world".

On a historic understanding of the episcopate the Bishop is the chief pastor and guardian of doctrine within his diocese in whom all legislative, judicial and administrative authority is vested.[3] Those aspects of authority are not to be separated from his pastorate but are means by which it may be exercised in the service of the people entrusted to his care. The Bishop's authority is moreover to be understood in the context of the general law of the Church with which any diocesan legislative, judicial or administrative act must consist. And insofar as they seek to bind the Church as a whole Bishops must act collegially. Thus the steps taken in the 18th century towards the reorganisation of the Church were initiated and carried through by the Bishops as a body and as legislators for the whole Church. That remains a fundamental of Episcopalian polity but, as can be seen from the course of subsequent developments, the governance of the Church is not to be exercised by the Bishops in isolation.

In contemplation of the Canon Law, unless where the Canons otherwise provide, the diocesan Bishop has original jurisdiction

---

[3] P A Lempriere, *A Compendium of the Canon Law for the Use of the Clergy and Theological Students of the Scottish Episcopal Church* (London and Oxford, 1903), p 57.

as judge ordinary of the bounds of his diocese and appellate jurisdiction is vested in the Episcopal Synod. The diocesan Bishop has in addition an appellate jurisdiction where the Canons or a relevant constitutive deed so provide and the Episcopal Synod has an original jurisdiction on similar principles and, more generally, in extra-diocesan and inter-diocesan matters.

5.4   Organisational Structure

5.4.1   *Episcopal Synod and College of Bishops; Election of Bishops*

The Episcopal Synod is an assembly of the diocesan Bishops duly convened and constituted in synod as must be done for the election of a Primus, the transaction of most judicial business and, in any event, at least once per year. When acting collegially or corporately, but less formally, they are known as the College of Bishops.

The Episcopal Synod elects one of its number as Primus to preside, except where other provision is made, at meetings of the Episcopal Synod, the College of Bishops and the General Synod, to carry out certain functions and duties assigned to his office by the Canons and to represent the Church in its relation to all other churches of the Anglican and other Communions.

The Scottish Episcopal Church, unlike its late medieval and Restoration predecessors, has no archbishops and the metropolitical powers which an archbishop would possess are vested in the College of Bishops. Those powers are the source of the appellate and original jurisdiction of the Episcopal Synod and of its legislative function now devolved to the General Synod.

The right to elect a Bishop when a see becomes vacant is vested in the Electoral Synod of the diocese which consists of two houses, one of the clerical members and the other of the lay members of the Diocesan Synod. The candidate elected must have a majority of votes in each house. The election is made from a list of candidates prepared by a committee consisting of the Primus as convener, one other Bishop and clerical and lay members representative both of the province as a whole and of the diocese. The assent of the College of Bishops is required for the inclusion of a candidate in the list.

5.4.2   *General Synod*

The membership of the General Synod consists of the diocesan Bishops, the conveners of certain provincial boards, the Principal of the Theological Institute, the representative of the Scottish

Episcopal Church on the Anglican Consultative Council and elected representatives, at present 140 in total, of the clergy and laity of the dioceses. The General Synod normally meets as one body but, when requested to do so by the majority of any house, meets in separate houses of Bishops, clergy and laity. Even when it meets as one body, votes in each house must for certain purposes be counted separately.

The General Synod has power to alter, modify, or abrogate any Canon or add to it and to enact new Canons. Any such proposal requires in the first instance to be passed by a simple majority of the members of each of the three houses present and voting. Thereafter the proposal must be submitted to Diocesan Synods for their comments and those comments considered by the General Synod at a subsequent meeting. The proposal, which may incorporate amendments not irrelevant to, beyond the scope of or inconsistent with the general subject matter and purport of the proposal as submitted to Diocesan Synods, may then be confirmed if passed by a two-thirds majority of the members of each house of the General Synod present and voting.

In addition to its powers in the alteration and enactment of Canons, the General Synod may by resolution provide for the implementation of the Canons, for procedures thereunder and for the regulation of its own procedure and of all matters of property, finance and general administration throughout the Church. Such resolutions, which may be passed by a simple majority of those present and voting at any meeting of the General Synod, must not be inconsistent with the Canons nor, except in so far as the Canons so provide or is necessary for their implementation or the regulation of procedures thereunder, encroach on any matter of doctrine, order or discipline or anything within the exclusive province of Bishops, the College of Bishops or the Episcopal Synod.

The General Synod has no judicial power either at first instance or on appeal.

5.4.3   Dioceses; Diocesan Synod

There are seven[4] dioceses each with a diocesan bishop who, subject to the laws of the Church and to the rights and duties conferred by those laws on other persons and bodies, is responsible for the governance of the diocese.

---

[4] Aberdeen and Orkney; Argyll and the Isles; Brechin; Edinburgh; Glasgow and Galloway; Moray, Ross and Caithness; and St Andrews, Dunblane and Dunkeld.

In every diocese there is a Diocesan Synod consisting of the Bishop, all instituted, licensed and commissioned clergy of the diocese, a lay representative for each congregation within the diocese, the lay members and alternate lay members of the General Synod elected by the Diocesan Synod and such additional lay members as the Diocesan Synod may elect. The synod must meet annually and in addition there may be special meetings for specified business whenever the Bishop sees cause. Clergy are obliged to attend and subject to sanction for failure. Meetings are presided over by the Bishop whom failing the Dean or in his absence by a member appointed by the meeting. No resolution of the Synod can receive effect if the Bishop intimates disagreement with it, but if the resolution is supported by two-thirds of the members present and qualified to vote an appeal if assented to by them is competent to the Episcopal Synod. Resolutions of the Diocesan Synod can in any event receive effect only in so far as they are within the competence of the Diocesan Synod and are not inconsistent with the Code of Canons or resolutions of the General Synod.

5.4.4 Cathedrals

In every diocese there is a Cathedral which is the principal or mother church of the diocese and in which the throne of the Bishop is situated. Every cathedral constituted after 1890 is governed by a code of statutes any breach of which may be dealt with in the same way as if it were a breach of the Code of Canons. The Bishop is head of the cathedral and its primary function is as the church of the Bishop but in all the Scottish cathedrals there is a cathedral congregation with an incumbent who is their Rector and usually, unless the Bishop himself assumes the office, Provost of the Cathedral. The rights and duties of the Provost are laid down in the statutes which in most cases provide that under the Bishop and with his concurrence the Provost governs the cathedral and controls the performance of all divine offices. In each cathedral there is a Cathedral Chapter the membership of which is prescribed in the statutes. The chapter constitutes the Bishop's council and its functions are now mainly as a source of consultation for and assistance to the Bishop.

5.4.5 Congregations

Subject to the Code of Canons, the Resolutions of the General Synod and any other relevant legislation and deeds, the general management of a congregation is regulated by its constitution.

There are four forms of congregations – incumbencies, joint incumbencies, linked charges and dependent congregations. In addition, some congregations, known as "independent congregations" under the provisions of earlier Canons now repealed, continue to enjoy that status on a transitional basis. For a congregation to be constituted as an incumbency it is essential that there be a church or suitable building for divine worship provided to the satisfaction of the Bishop, that a constitution be sanctioned by the Bishop and that there should be compliance with certain requirements as to title deeds of property and provision for the maintenance of the ministry. The cleric to whom the pastoral charge of an incumbency is committed is known as the Rector.

When an incumbency becomes vacant the right of presentation is to be exercised by the person or persons in whom that right is vested (the patrons) as determined by the constitution of the congregation or other constitutive document. The Vestry or Bishop or some combination of them ("Vestry in consultation with the Bishop" or "Bishop and Vestry") is commonly the patron. In any event the Bishop may refuse a presentation but, if he does so, an appeal is competent to the Episcopal Synod.

Two or more congregations may form a joint incumbency if they desire to be linked together under a joint constitution with a joint Rector, a joint Vestry and a single set of office-bearers. The participating congregations retain a separate identity to the extent that there is a lay representative to the Diocesan Synod for each participating congregation and that individual charges within the joint incumbency may create sub-committees of the joint Vestry to deal with matters which relate to them.

Where two or more incumbencies wish to collaborate in order to provide for ministry and are unable, for reasons considered sufficient by the Bishop, to form a joint incumbency, they may instead form a linked charge under one Rector and subject to a minute of agreement setting out terms of co-operation.

Where a church or other building in addition to the original or mother church is provided for public worship within a district assigned to a charge the members and communicants attending that church may form a dependent congregation. They are deemed to be members and communicants of the mother church, with all the rights and privileges attaching to that including the election of a lay representative to the Diocesan Synod unless, if certain conditions are satisfied, the Bishop and a majority of members present in Diocesan Synod and qualified to vote assent to their electing a separate lay representative.

5.4.6   *Vestries*

The Vestry is the managing body of a congregation. Its composition is as laid down in the constitution of the congregation
and invariably includes the Rector as a member *ex officio* and
chair and members elected by the congregation in its annual
general meeting. The lay representative of the congregation in the
Diocesan Synod is also a member *ex officio* unless the constitution
otherwise provides and where there are church wardens the
Rector's Warden and the People's Warden will also usually be
members. The temporal affairs and finances of the congregation
are in the hands of the Vestry and members of the Vestry will
normally be regarded as "charity trustees" for the purposes, here
applicable, of the Charities and Trustee Investment (Scotland)
Act 2005. Unless the duty has been placed on Church Wardens,
the Vestry is required along with the Rector to have care of the
property and fabric of the church and, unless otherwise directed,
of gifts and bequests. It is also required to co-operate with and
generally assist the Rector in all matters relating to the spiritual
welfare of the congregation and the mission of the whole church,
subject always to the canonical rights and duties of the clergy.[5]

5.5   The Law of the Church

5.5.1   *The Code of Canons; Canon Law*

For the purposes of most disputes coming before the judicial
bodies of the Church the applicable law can be found in the Code
of Canons and its subordinate legislation.[6] The Code of Canons
is a development and reformulation, in the light of subsequent
experience and theological reflection, of those aspects of the pre-
Reformation Canon Law deemed relevant to the circumstances of
the Scottish Episcopal Church. In the matters to which it refers the
Code supersedes the pre-Reformation law and beyond that there
is little scope for the direct application of the pre-Reformation
law, at least in its substantive aspects. Awareness of the pre-
Reformation heritage and of its principles and jurisprudence
underlies, however, a proper understanding and interpretation of
the Code of Canons.

It is also necessary to bring to the task of interpretation of the
Code an understanding of the sources of Canon Law. Principal

---

[5] Canon 60. See also Model Constitution.
[6] Ie the resolutions and rules of the General Synod and other bodies to which
rule-making power has been given expressly or impliedly by the Code of Canons
or delegated by resolution within the canonical powers of the General Synod.

among these are scripture, tradition and natural law, all of which have been formative in the shaping of the Canons and remain fundamental to their interpretation.

5.5.2 Scripture

Lempriere considered the moral law of the Old Testament (as distinct from the ceremonial or judicial law) to be still in force and the precepts of the Gospel to be the foundation of Canon Law.[7] Modern scholarship and theological understanding make the use of scripture in interpretation of the Canons a more complex and more difficult task than it may have appeared to Lempriere a century ago. In cases to which provisions of the Code of Canons properly and unambiguously apply no question of interpretation arises. They are to be taken, as long as they stand, to represent in their terms the mind of the Church on the translation of scripture into legal principle. Where, however, there is room for interpretation scripture properly understood remains an essential guide. The Code is to be interpreted in the light of the message of the Gospel which it exists to serve.

5.5.3 Tradition

Considerations similar to those applying to scripture apply to tradition. The tradition of the universal church going back to the Apostles is a primary source of Canon Law and remains relevant to its interpretation. There may, however, be problems of discernment, not unlike those which arise in relation to scripture, as to what is essential and what is peripheral or in need of reconsideration and reform. To earlier tradition should now be added the tradition of the Anglican Communion of which the Episcopal Church is a member. Resolutions of the Lambeth Conferences of Anglican Bishops and other pronouncements on behalf of the worldwide Anglican Communion although not of binding authority are to be taken into account in any interpretation of the Canons.

5.5.4 Natural law

The precepts of natural law in the sense of the principles of equity and justice implanted by reason in the human conscience are, like scripture and tradition, to be regarded as of divine origin and to be implicit in the Canons. They have continuing significance not

---

[7] Above n 3, p 2.

least in supplying the requirement of compliance with the rules of natural justice in canonical processes for which no procedural requirements are laid down.

5.5.5   Extra-canonical sources of law

Although the Code of Canons and its subordinate legislation are sufficient, if properly understood and interpreted, for the resolution of most disputes, it is error to regard them as exhaustive of the law of the Church. The modern trend has been to expand the scope of canonical enactment but there remain many matters particularly in relation to doctrine, order and liturgy which find no place in the Code of Canons but form an undoubted part of the law of the Church. Rules on these matters are to be found in the approved formularies and usage of the Church and where not defined can still be the subject of definition by the College of Bishops in exercise of their Episcopal authority. And the mere absence of canonical provision does not determine the legitimacy of a matter which may require consideration of scripture and tradition.

5.6   Church and State

5.6.1   Ecclesiastical law of the State

Those parts of the law of Scotland which apply specifically to churches may be described as ecclesiastical law and are part of the secular legal system. They should not be confused with the law of the Church, which consists of its internal rules, or superimposed as if part of it. That the law of the State is part of the law of the Church may be true of established churches if, even there, subject to some qualification. In relation to Churches outwith the state system it is misleading. The law of the Church, as well as counsels of prudence and morality, may in general require compliance with the law of the State but, unless where the law of the Church so indicates, that is a different matter from saying that the law of the State, however benign, is imported into the law of the Church.[8] If the law of the State clashes with the law of the Church or with the Christian conscience, the separate nature and sources of the two systems are evident.

---

[8] Lempriere's view (above, n 3, p 30) that the Church had assented to the limitation of its independence according to the common law of the realm is based on a provision in the Code of Canons of 1890 which has been repealed and which, it is submitted, was misconceived.

5.6.2 Legal status of the Church

The Scottish Episcopal Church is in contemplation of the law of Scotland an unincorporated religious association marked off from other voluntary churches only by the distinct legal regulation to which Scottish Episcopalians were for long subject. The Bishops and other judicatories of the Episcopal Church do not have jurisdiction in the full sense of judicial power conferred by the state and as enjoyed by the courts of the Church of Scotland as ecclesiastical courts of the realm.[9] They may, however, have a contractual jurisdiction implicit in the contract of association constituted by membership of the Church and as such recognised by the civil law.[10]

Parts of the Scottish Episcopalians Act 1711 remain in force but do not affect the legal status of the Church which is governed by the law generally applicable to voluntary religious associations. For a full discussion of the applicable law, which falls outwith the scope of this work, reference should be made to the relevant legal texts.[11]

---

[9] *Dunbar* v *Skinner* (1849) 11 D 945; cf *MacMillan* v *General Assembly of the Free Church of Scotland* (1859) 22 D 290 per Lord Deas at 323.
[10] *McDonald* v *Burns* 1940 SC 376 per LJ-C Aitchison at 382.
[11] A B Wilkinson, "The Scottish Episcopal Church", *Stair Memorial Encyclopedia of the Laws of Scotland*, vol 3, pp 764–779, paras 1610–1631. See also *ibid* P Brodie and Lord Mackay of Clashfern, "Voluntary Churches", pp 779–801, paras 1632–1653; and F Lyall, "Of Presbyters and Kings" (Aberdeen, 1980), pp 85–112.

CHAPTER 6

SCOTTISH EPISCOPAL CHURCH: JUDICIAL PROCEDURES I – GENERAL

A B WILKINSON

6.1 Introduction

This chapter deals with the various situations to which the law of the Scottish Episcopal Church may be applied and with the procedures for the resolution of disputes by judicial or quasi-judicial means. Sufficient information has, it is hoped, been given for an initial appreciation of the issues involved. No attempt has, however, been made at a full statement of the law and reference should always be made to the Code of Canons and other applicable legislation for a legal assessment of the merits of any given case. Copies of the Code of Canons and other relevant information may be obtained from the General Synod office at:

General Synod of the Scottish Episcopal Church
21 Grosvenor Crescent
Edinburgh EH12 5EE
(telephone: 0131 225 6357; fax: 0131 346 7247)

The right of parties to legal representation is specifically affirmed by the Canons in a number of situations. In others it will usually be allowed where appropriate.

No form of address or dress code is laid down for lawyers or others appearing before the judicial bodies of the Church. It is, however, usual and appropriate in appearances before the Episcopal Synod to address the bench as "My Lords", to refer to them as "Your Lordships" and generally to conduct oneself as one would before a court of law. Similarly, in formal appearances before a Bishop and in answering questions from an individual member of the Episcopal Synod, "My Lord" and "Your Lordship" are appropriate. On less formal occasions a Bishop may be addressed as "Bishop" and the Primus as "Primus".

Tribunals and committees of the church are addressed through the chair in the usual way. Court gowns are not usually worn before any of the judicial bodies of the Church. For lawyers, suits for men and equivalent dress for women are appropriate. For written communications the appropriate style for the Primus is "The Most Reverend the Primus of the Scottish Episcopal Church" and for Bishops "The Right Reverend the Bishop of [name of diocese]".

6.2   Resolution of Situations of Pastoral Breakdown (Canon 53)

The pastoral care of the people committed to his charge is a fundamental part of the ministry to which a priest or deacon is called and the maintenance of a pastoral relationship with them a fundamental duty. Both the authority and the responsibility to exercise the pastorate are, however, derived from and shared with the Bishop as chief pastor of the diocese and on instituting an incumbent the Bishop reserves to himself and all his successors in the Episcopal office the right to perform all pastoral duties in the incumbency.[1] The right reserved to the Bishop is unrestricted in its scope and thus includes, although is not confined to, intervention in cases of pastoral difficulty; and the maintenance of the pastoral relationship between a cleric and the congregation committed to his charge is a concern of the Bishop no less than of the cleric.[2] Accordingly, in the event of the breakdown or threatened breakdown of that relationship it is part of the ordinary duties of the Bishop to seek to restore the relationship. Canon 53 envisages that recourse should generally be, at least in the first instance, to measures, usually informal, within the ordinary powers of the Bishop. Where, however, the breakdown is perceived to be of such extent that the relationship cannot be restored in that way, specific provision is made for further and formal canonical procedures to resolve the situation.

6.2.1   Request for inquiry; notice of intention

The procedure for resolution of a perceived situation of pastoral breakdown is by way of request to the diocesan Bishop for an inquiry, preceded by a notice in writing advising the Bishop of the intention to make the request.

---

[1] Code of Canons, Appendix 14.
[2] Canon 53, s 1.

The notice of intention must be given at least 6 months and no more than 12 months before the request itself is made. The procedure may be initiated by:

(a) the cleric in charge of the congregation concerned; or

(b) a majority of at least two-thirds of the lay membership of the Vestry of that congregation present and voting at a specially convened meeting; or

(c) the Synod Clerk of the diocese or, if he is involved in the perceived breakdown, the Dean.

There is no definition of what constitutes a "perceived situation of pastoral breakdown" but the perception of the person or persons intending to make the request appears to be sufficient.

6.2.2   Discussion and conciliation

Upon receipt of the notice the Bishop is required to attempt to resolve the matter by discussion with the parties concerned and must explain to them the implications and possible consequences of a formal inquiry. If reconciliation by such discussion is impossible the Bishop must, with the agreement of the parties, appoint a conciliator who, by means of interview and the institution of dialogue, is to attempt to bring the matter to resolution within 6 months of the notice of intention. If the conciliator should fail to bring about a resolution he must submit a report to the Bishop of the steps that have been taken, any progress made and the extent of co-operation of each of the parties.

6.2.3   Failure of conciliation and reception of request

If conciliation fails or if it has been impossible to appoint a conciliator, whether from the failure of the parties to agree to an appointment or other cause, the Bishop has discretion to take further steps before receiving the request for an inquiry. It is unclear whether these words imply a power in the Bishop to delay reception of a request but any lengthy delay would, it is submitted, be an abuse of power inconsistent with the overall scheme of the Canon and destructive of its purposes. In constrast with the notice of intention, there is no requirement that the request should be in writing, although it is clearly desirable that that should be so.

6.2.4   Report by Dean – further action

On receiving a request for an inquiry the Bishop is to require the Dean of the diocese to report within 6 months upon whether an inquiry would be in the interests of the incumbent and of the congregation.[3] It appears from later provisions that the Dean is also to make a recommendation on the appropriateness of an inquiry.[4] No test of appropriateness is laid down but it may be assumed to be based on the Dean's assessment of interests. The question of a possible conflict of interest is not addressed but where there is such a conflict it is submitted that an inquiry will often be appropriate. The matter is, however, at large for the Dean to determine.

If the Report recommends that an inquiry is appropriate one, of three courses of action is available to the Bishop. He may:

(1) institute a hearing by the Provincial Advisory Board on Pastoral Breakdown; or

(2) notwithstanding the Report, dismiss the matter; or

(3) recommend that the matter is of sufficient seriousness that proceedings under Canon 54 (clergy discipline) are appropriate.

There is no provision as to what should happen if the Report does not recommend that an inquiry would be appropriate but it appears that the request for an inquiry should either be allowed to lapse or, perhaps better, be dismissed.

6.2.5 Inquiry by Provincial Advisory Board

Where the Bishop, having decided that an inquiry is appropriate, institutes a hearing by the Provincial Advisory Board on Pastoral Breakdown, the parties must, within 12 months of the receipt by the Bishop of the notice of intention to make a request for an inquiry, present their cases to the Board.[5] There is no provision regulating the procedure before the Board but it is implicit in the Canon, as in all canonical procedures, that the rules of natural justice must be observed. If the Board makes inquiries at its own hand they should therefore be communicated to the parties and the parties given an opportunity of being heard

---

[3] S 5. If the Dean should be disqualified because he is a party to the matter, the Synod Clerk is to act in his place; if both should be disqualified the Bishop is to require another cleric of good standing within the diocese to take their place.

[4] S 6.

[5] S 7. The Board consists of persons chosen when required by the College of Bishops from members of the Clergy Discipline Tribunal. The number of persons to be chosen is not specified and appears to be at the discretion of the College of Bishops.

on them. An oral hearing appears to be contemplated and, in any event, will usually be necessary in the nature of the case. Having completed its inquiry the Board is required to make recommendations to the Bishop on the appropriate means of resolving the situation.

6.2.6   Action following Report by Provincial Advisory Board

Following the Report of the Board, which the Bishop at his discretion may or may not make public, the Bishop is required to provide pastoral advice to the cleric and the Vestry as seems appropriate. He may also:

(a) if, but only if, the Board so advises, declare the cleric's charge vacant at a specific date;[6]

(b) rebuke the cleric or any other cleric and, at his discretion, disqualify him from the performance of specified duties for a specified period;

(c) rebuke a member or members of the congregation and disqualify them from holding office within the congregation or the diocese for a period not exceeding 5 years.

The powers of rebuke and disqualification in relation to both cleric and members of the congregation may be exercised whether or not the Board so recommends.

6.2.7   Appeal

Within 1 month of the Bishop's decision, any party may appeal against it to the Episcopal Synod. The procedure and rights of parties before the Episcopal Synod are as described below under "Other Disputes and Differences".

6.3   Physical or Mental Incapacity of Clergy (Canon 64)

6.3.1   Referral to Medical Review Panel

The physical or mental incapacity of clergy is in the first instance to be dealt with pastorally by the diocesan Bishop, any other clergy concerned and the Vestry of the congregation in which the cleric exercises ministerial duties. Canon 64 provides, however,

---

[6] Before making such a declaration the Bishop may recommend in an appropriate case that the cleric undergo a medical examination to determine his fitness to continue.

for situations in which a formal procedure is desirable. In such cases referral may be made to the Medical Review Panel of the circumstances of a cleric who, in the opinion of the Bishop or Dean of the diocese, has become unfit to fulfil the responsibilities of the ministry.[7] The Bishop must, moreover, make such a referral if requested to do so by the cleric himself or, in writing, by the Vestry.[8]

6.3.2   Assessment procedure

On referral to the Medical Review Panel an assessment panel chosen from its members is required to conduct an independent assessment with a view to determining whether the cleric referred to it is fit to fulfil the responsibilities of the ministry currently entrusted to him.[9] The assessment procedure includes the obtaining of medical reports, a meeting between the cleric and an independent assessor chosen from the members of the panel and a meeting between the cleric and the assessment panel itself to which, as well as to any subsequent meeting, the cleric may bring two persons to support him, one of whom may be legally qualified.[10] No legal representations are, however, to be entertained.[11] Submissions may therefore be made on questions of fact but not of law. Failure to attend a meeting of the assessment panel may result in suspension without stipend.[12]

6.3.3   Decision of assessment panel

Following the conclusion of its meeting with the cleric, or of a subsequent meeting if that is required, the assessment panel may reach a decision as to the cleric's fitness for ministry. The decision, which must be accompanied by a written Report outlining reasons, may be to the effect that:

(a) the cleric's fitness for ministry is satisfactory; or

(b) the cleric's ministerial duties should be reduced to a specified level; or

---

[7] Ss 2 and 4(a). Where the person to be referred is a Bishop the entitlement to a make a referral vests in the Primus, whom failing, the senior Bishop.
[8] S 4(b) and (c).
[9] S 3.
[10] Ss 5, 6 and 7.
[11] S 7.
[12] S 9. The Bishop or, where the cleric suspended is a Bishop, the Primus is to make appropriate pastoral and financial arrangements for the cleric's immediate family.

(c) the cleric should be required to undertake a period of leave from ministerial duties (with or without sick leave payment); or

(d) in the light of his physical or mental health, the cleric is unfit to continue in his current ministerial post.[13]

In reaching any decision the panel may in addition recommend that the cleric attend a specified course of treatment or counselling of which the costs will be met by the Church. Where the decision is that the cleric's ministerial duties should be reduced the diocesan Bishop is to appoint a person to supervise that reduction. In the case of decisions (c) or (d) above the Bishop must ensure that the cleric and his immediate family are provided with appropriate pastoral and financial support.

6.3.4 Appeals and review

An appeal lies to the Episcopal Synod against the appointment by the Bishop of any particular individual to supervise reduction of ministerial duties (and to the Bishop and thereafter to the Episcopal Synod against any unreasonable directions given by that person); and the cleric and any member of his immediate family affected by the decision may appeal to the Episcopal Synod as to the reasonableness of any assessment made by the Bishop of appropriate pastoral and financial support.

Appeal also lies to the Episcopal Synod against a decision by the assessment panel to suspend a cleric for failing to meet with them.

All other appeals against decisions by the assessment panel, whether at the instance of the cleric or of the person or body who made the referral, must be made to an appeal panel consisting of three members of the Medical Review Panel other than those who constituted the assessment panel. The appeal panel must review the decision appealed against and may affirm it or set it aside and make an alternative decision. The appeal must be in writing and made within 21 days of the assessment panel's decision. There is

---

[13] Ss 8 and 9. Where the cleric concerned is a Bishop it is for the Episcopal Synod to appoint a person to supervise any reduction in his duties and, where a decision under para (c) or (d) has been made, to ensure the provision of appropriate pastoral and financial support. Where the cleric is required to undertake a period of leave or attend a course of treatment or counselling the assessment panel will meet with him shortly before the end of the period of leave or, after a reasonable time has elapsed for attendance at the course, to assess whether the cleric is then fit to return to duties.

no provision for an oral hearing or further inquiry and it appears that the appeal panel's review is to be carried out on the basis of the written submissions in the appeal, the assessment panel's reasons and the reports and other evidence previously obtained.

No appeal is competent in respect of the findings of the appeal panel as to the state of the cleric's physical or mental health, but appeal may be taken to the Episcopal Synod against any direction made by the appeal panel that a period of leave recommended by it should be unpaid or that a cleric is unfit to continue in his current ministerial post.

6.4   Protection of Children and Vulnerable Adults (Canon 65)

Canon 65 and associated Church policies and subordinate legislation are to be understood in the context of widespread public concern about the abuse of children and vulnerable adults and of legislation and government policy designed for their protection.

6.4.1   *Interpretation – criminal record disclosure and decisions on fitness*

The Provincial Officer for the Protection of Children and Vulnerable Adults has authority to apply for criminal record disclosures in respect of any persons holding, applying for or proposed for a post within the Church whose work may bring them into contact with children or vulnerable adults. He also has authority to make decisions in relation to the fitness of any person or body to be appointed to a post within the Church involving work with or having access to children or vulnerable adults.[14] On complex and difficult questions regarding the suitability of any person or body he has a duty to seek the advice of the Provincial Committee for the Protection of Children and Vulnerable Adults.

The disclosures contemplated, although not so expressed in the Canon, are those to be obtained by application to Disclosure Scotland in pursuance of Part V of the Police Act 1997. In accordance with policies adopted by the Church, and consistently with the Act, the application will be made not by the Provincial Officer but by the person seeking appointment to or holding a post.[15] The authority to apply given to the Provincial Officer

---

[14] Canon 65, ss 3 and 4.
[15] See Code of Practice for Registered Persons and Other Recipients of Disclosure Information promulgated by Disclosure Scotland and adopted by the General Synod in June, 2002. See also *Scottish Episcopal Church Child Protection Handbook*.

appears to be a matter of ensuring that application in proper form is made.

No definition is given in the Canon of what is meant by "children" or "vulnerable adults" but it is necessary in the context that they should bear the same meaning as in State legislation.[16] Other difficulties of interpretation remain. Application by the Provinical Officer for disclosure is to be made in respect of, among others, "any persons holding a post" but his authority to make a decision is only in respect of fitness "to be appointed to a post". Resolutions of the General Synod may, however, supply the resultant gap.[17]

6.4.2 *Decisions on fitness – intimation, review and effect*

If the Provincial Officer decides that a person is not suitable to hold or to continue to hold an appointment that decision should be intimated in writing to the person affected who may ask for a review of the decision. If a written request for a review is made within 28 days of the posting of the notice of decision, the Provincial Officer must reconsider the decision complained of, make a further decision and send to the applicant a written statement of the reasons, taking into account representations made, for the further decision.[18]

All decisions taken by the Provincial Officer are binding upon all persons or bodies to whom they relate, subject only to appeal to the Provincial Appeals Committee for the Protection of Children and Vulnerable Adults.[19] The result is that, subject to such appeal, no appointment to a post can be made of a person who is found to be unfit for appointment by the Provincial Officer and any purported appointment is *ultra vires* and null. A similar result ensues in cases of persons in post.

6.4.3 *Appeal*

Appeal to the Appeals Committee lies solely in relation to a decision made with reference to the question of fitness for

---

[16] Protection of Children (Scotland) Act 2003, s 18 (person under the age of 18), the Police Act 1997 (Enhanced Criminal Records Certificates) (Protection of Vulnerable Adults) (Scotland) Regulations 2002 (a person who in consequence of a learning or physical disability, a physical or mental illness or a reduction in physical or mental capacity has a disability of a listed type for which he or she is receiving services of a type listed in the regulations). "Adult" in terms of the Canons means of person who has attained the age of 18 years (Canon 57).

[17] Resolution 1 made under Canon 65. See also Schedule to the Canon.

[18] Review Procedures, para 1.

[19] Canon 65, s 5.

appointment arising from information contained in the criminal record disclosure relating to the appellant.[20] An affected person dissatisfied with the Provincial Officer's decision, whether or not after review, may appeal against that decision by written intimation of appeal to the Secretary General of the General Synod.[21]

Appeals are heard at an oral hearing by a panel consisting of three members of the Appeals Committee selected by the Clerk to the Committee. The chairperson must be legally qualified and the panel is not to consist solely of male or solely of female members.[22] The appellant has a right to be represented and the right (whether personally or through his legal representative) to address the panel first.[23] Beyond that, no rules for the conduct of the proceedings are laid down which, subject to the rules of natural justice, is at the discretion of the panel. The decision of the Appeals Committee is final and further appeal to the Episcopal Synod is expressly excluded.[24]

6.5   Repelling from Holy Communion (Canon 26)

Where a person is living in open and unrepented sin it is the inherent right of the Bishop of the diocese to repel him or her from Holy Communion. The priest of the church where the case occurs should, without delay, give a warning to the person concerned and if he or she is unrepentant should report the whole matter to the Bishop and proceed thereafter as the Bishop may direct. In a case of unforeseen urgency the priest may refuse communion until the matter can be brought before the Bishop. In deciding the case, the Bishop must observe any regulations made by the College of Bishops and before giving his decision give the person alleged to have offended an opportunity of being heard.[25] If, before making his decision, the Bishop consults the College of Bishops, as he is entitled to do, the College must make such reasonable inquiry as they think right and the Bishop must follow their opinion.[26]

No further appeal is allowed if the Bishop has consulted the College of Bishops before making his decision. If, however, that

---

[20] Canon 65, s 7.
[21] For time limits, see Appeals Procedures, paras 2 and 3.
[22] *Ibid*, para 5.
[23] *Ibid*, para 8.
[24] Canon 65, s 7.
[25] Canon 26, s 2.
[26] S 3.

has not been done, a person repelled from Holy Communion may require the Bishop to consult the College of Bishops as to whether or not the order of repulsion should be recalled and the Bishop must give effect to the opinion which the College gives after such informal inquiry as they think right.[27] There is no canonical provision for affording a hearing in connection with a request for recall but it may be pastorally appropriate for the Bishop, or for the College of Bishops as part of its inquiry, to do so.

It is submitted that the provisions for request for recall relate to the situation obtaining at the time the Bishop's decision was made and that in the event of repentance or any relevant change of circumstances the Bishop as Ordinary of the diocese has an inherent right to recall the order, provided that any regulations made by the College of Bishops are followed and the recall is not inconsistent with any opinion they have given in the case.

6.6   Property

The Church, in contemplation of the secular law, belongs to that class of voluntary association which exists for purposes or objects which extend beyond the material or social benefit of its members. As a result the general principles of trust law, rather than the law of joint property and contract applicable to a social club, govern the management and application of its funds and property. Canon law, if on different reasoning, points to a similar result. Moreover, much Church property is held on specific trusts, whether for general or for particular Church purposes, to which the law of trusts plainly applies.

The Code of Canons provides that nothing in the Canons "shall be construed as empowering the General Synod to alter the terms of any Deed of Trust or the terms on which any property outwith its control is held". However, the General Synod has power to provide by resolution for the regulation of *inter alia* the holding of property under trust. It follows that if a trust has been set up by the General Synod for the management of property under its unrestricted control, the General Synod may itself alter the terms of that trust on the principles generally applicable to revocable trusts. In general, however, if trust purposes fail or if a question arises of reorganising a trust in a way which necessitates the alteration of its terms, a solution can be achieved only by resort to the civil courts or to the statutory procedures for reorganisation of trusts.

---

[27] *Ibid.*

The management of trust property is a matter for the trustees. However, if the trust deed so provides, appeal on any matter relating to the trust may be pursued, as noted below, under the procedure provided by Canon 53 unless a special appeal procedure is provided in terms of the deed. It may also be possible to seek a resolution of disputes about property under the provisions of Canon 53 on disputes as to questions affecting congregations, dioceses or the Province if the deed of trust can be construed as providing for such resolution or where property is held on constructive trust or where the parties so agree.

6.7   Structure, Furniture and Monuments of Churches (Canon 35)

Canon 35 contains restrictions, which extend to schemes of re-decoration and alterations in heating and lighting systems, on changes to the structure, ecclesiastical furniture and monuments of any church used for public worship. No such change, other than experimental re-ordering of ecclesiastical furniture and ornaments, may be made unless the Vestry, with the consent of the Rector, obtains the approval in writing of the Bishop and of the Diocesan Buildings Advisory Committee. The approval given by the Bishop and the diocesan advisory committee must be in terms which do not violate any restrictions contained in the constitution or titles of the Church. There is a right of appeal to the Provincial Buildings Advisory Committee from decisions of the diocesan committee or the Bishop at the instance of the Vestry or 20 per cent of the members on the Communicants' Roll. The decision of the Provincial Buildings Advisory Committee is final.[28]

6.8   Resolution of Other Disputes and Differences (Canon 53)

In addition to providing for cases of pastoral breakdown Canon 53, in separate provisions, affords means for resolution of other disputes and differences. The procedure it lays down applies, unless specific provision for a special appeal procedure has been made, to:

(1) all appeals to the Bishop of a diocese or the Episcopal Synod other than appeals relating to clergy discipline under Canon 54. Appeals falling under this heading include, for example, appeals relating to an Episcopal election

---

[28] Resolution 5 made under Canon 35.

(Canon 4, s 34), or to rejection of a presentation to an incumbency (Canon 13, ss 6 and 7) or to the constitution of a congregation as an incumbency under Canon 36 or to cases of clerical incapacity under Canon 64;

(2) appeals which may be made in terms of the constitution of any congregation or body relating to the Scottish Episcopal church or any part of it or in terms of any trust or other deed similarly applying; and

(3) all disputes between clergy or other members of the church as to questions affecting congregations, dioceses or the Province other than those relating to clergy discipline or cases of pastoral breakdown.[29]

All such appeals and disputes are to be referred to the Bishop of the Diocese in which the appeal or dispute arises or, if the Bishop is directly concerned or the matter is extra-diocesan or affects more than one diocese, to the Episcopal Synod.[30] As these words apply only where no "specific provision for a special appeal procedure" has been made, they do not derogate from any right of appeal directly to the Episcopal Synod given by any other canonical enactment or by any trust or other deed, nor, contrary to the general rule,[31] do they supersede any such right given by the constitution of any congregation or other body. In cases where the Bishop of the Diocese is concerned, the Episcopal Synod may, at the request of any of the parties involved, appoint another Bishop to act in his place and with the same powers as the Bishop of the Diocese.

In dealing with references to him the Bishop of the Diocese has full power and absolute discretion to regulate procedure, to hear parties or to dispense with hearing them, to require parties to submit their contentions orally or in writing, to take such evidence as seems fit to him, formally or informally, and generally to deal with the appeal and control the process of the hearing.[32] He remains, of course, bound by the rules of natural justice. His decision is final unless there is express provision under the applicable Canon, constitution or deed for appeal to the Episcopal Synod or he allows leave to appeal or, in the event of his refusal of

---

[29] Canon 53, s 10.
[30] *Ibid*, s 11.
[31] By Canon 58, the terms of the Canons supersede, in the event of inconsistency, the provisions of the constitution of any charge or diocese. The same rule does not apply to trusts.
[32] Canon, 53 s 12.

leave, leave is granted by the Episcopal Synod. If leave to appeal is required, application for leave must be made to the Bishop within 1 month of his decision. If the Bishop refuses the application, application for leave may be made to the Episcopal Synod within 1 month of that refusal and must be in writing addressed to the Clerk of the Episcopal Synod.[33]

Parties are entitled to be legally represented before the Episcopal Synod which has full power to regulate its own procedure, to hear parties or to dispense with hearing them, to require parties to submit their contentions orally or in writing, to take such evidence as seems fit to it, formally or informally, and generally to deal with the appeal and control the process.[34]

---

[33] S 13.
[34] S 14.

CHAPTER 7

SCOTTISH EPISCOPAL CHURCH: JUDICIAL PROCEDURES II – CLERGY DISCIPLINE, OFFENCES AND ACCUSATIONS (CANON 54)

A B WILKINSON

7.1 Introduction

The commission of an alleged offence by a member of the clergy is a matter for the pastoral concern of the diocesan Bishop no less than a case of breakdown of a pastoral relationship. However, the difficulty of reconciling pastoral and judicial functions arises more sharply than in cases unaffected by offending. The Bishop has to be mindful that his pastoral concern is for people whose interests may be in conflict; for the member of the clergy alleged to have offended, for people who may have been harmed and for the welfare of the Church as a whole. Accordingly, Canon 54, while expressing preference for complaints against clergy involving alleged offences to be dealt with pastorally by the Bishop, recognises that the pastoral resolution of a complaint or dispute may not be achieved and that recourse should then be had to rules for the good order of the Church and the discipline of the clergy.

Any accused person may be legally represented at a trial or appeal under this Canon.

7.2 Offences

Any of the following constitutes an offence where committed by a Priest or Deacon or, with the exception of paragraph (e) below, by a Bishop:

(a) behaviour or conduct in a manner unbecoming a member of the clergy, or in a way which causes or is likely to cause scandal or to bring the Church into disrepute. Such behaviour or conduct may include but is not limited to,

(i) behaviour or conduct which is the subject of a criminal conviction by a secular court;

(ii) sexual immorality or gross indecency;

(iii) habitual abuse of alcohol or other drugs.

(b) habitual or wilful neglect of the duties of clerical office, or of any position of trust or responsibility connected with such office to which the offender has been appointed or elected, or habitual carelessness or gross inefficiency in the discharge of such office.

(c) knowing violation of the Code of Canons or of anything lawfully ordered thereunder.

(d) teaching or publicly advocating doctrines or beliefs subversive of or incompatible with the teaching of the Church as expressed in its formularies.

(e) disobedience of Episcopal authority, or conduct or behaviour disrespectful to or showing contempt for the diocesan Bishop.[1]

7.3   Accusation

Procedure is by way of accusation which may be brought by any person admitted or entitled to be admitted[2] to the Roll of Communicants of a congregation or by the Provincial Officer for the Protection of Children and Vulnerable Adults.[3] The accusation may be brought against a Bishop, Priest or Deacon holding any form of authorisation to minister in the Scottish Episcopal Church whether temporary or non-temporary[4] and must be in writing setting out in detail, in respect of each offence and each cleric against whom an accusation is made:

(a) the offence allegedly committed,

(b) the name of the cleric concerning whom the allegation is made together with such other information concerning the identity of the cleric as is known to the complainer,

(c) the conduct complained of and how it is alleged to constitute an offence,

---

[1] Canon 54, s 2.

[2] In terms of Canon 41, s 2.

[3] S 3 of Canon 54. One would have expected any accusation brought by the Provincial Officer for the Protection of Children and Vulnerable Adults, who need not be a communicant member of the Church, to be confined to matters within his or her remit, but no such limitation is stated.

[4] S 3 read with s 6.

(d) the date or dates and place or places of the alleged commission of the offence where known,

(e) the basis of the complainer's knowledge of the alleged offence or where the facts are not within the personal knowledge of the complainer the grounds on which he or she believes the alleged offence to have taken place.

7.4 Preliminary Proceedings Committee

All accusations must be lodged in writing with the Secretary to the Preliminary Proceedings Committee which is a Committee of the General Synod constituted to investigate all accusations and consisting of three members appointed every 5 years by the General Synod[5] and two members, a diocesan Bishop[6] and a cleric of the same order as the accused cleric,[7] appointed for each accusation as it arises. Where an accusation is made concerning more than one cleric and they are of different orders, the clerical member of the Committee must be a priest.[8]

7.4.1 *Preliminary consideration and investigation*

The purpose for which the Committee is constituted is the investigation of accusations,[9] but its functions extend to considering the results of its investigations and deciding on further procedure.[10] There is no specific provision for dealing with issues of competency and legal relevancy but it is submitted that, if such questions appear on the face of the accusation or if it appears that the accusation may be frivolous, the Committee sufficiently discharges its investigative function by giving the complainer an opportunity to be heard and thereafter coming to a decision on whether investigation on the merits is required.

The way in which the Committee is to consider an accusation and carry out its investigations is largely left to its discretion.

---

[5] Two practising lawyers, one at least being an admitted solicitor, and a lay person who is an adult communicant member of the Church.
[6] Nominated by the College of Bishops.
[7] Appointed by the standing committee of the General Synod.
[8] S 5. A member is disqualified by close personal or business connection with the accused and, with the exception of the two lawyer members, by residence or holding office in the same diocese at the time of the alleged offence. There is provision for appointing alternates to serve in place of disqualified members, for filling casual vacancies and for ensuring continuity of membership throughout the investigation.
[9] *Ibid.*

Certain matters are, however, laid down. If at any time in considering an accusation the Committee finds that no offence has been committed it should determine that no further action should be taken and notify the accused persons, the complainers and the diocesan Bishop accordingly.[11] Accusations concerning more than one cleric may, if related in time, place, nature or manner of misconduct, be considered and investigated together.[12] Moreover, if in the course of its investigation the Committee finds evidence of an offence which is not included in the original accusation, it is to proceed to consider the evidence of that offence and to investigate it as if an accusation of that offence had been made.[13] The Committee has power to take statements from witnesses and to request sight and retention of all documents held by any person or body within or on behalf of the Church and any such person or body must allow sight of them or deliver them up if requested to do so.[14] Failure by a cleric to respond to such a request may itself be an offence under the Canon[15] but there is no ecclesiastical sanction which can readily be invoked against non-compliance by lay persons. The Canons are, however, binding on lay members of the Church as well as clergy[16] and civil remedies may be available against both clergy and laity for recovery of documents unlawfully withheld in breach of the obligation implicit in membership.

Until the Committee has completed its investigation no response is required or, it seems, to be expected or invited from the accused person or persons. Within 2 weeks of the completion of its investigation the Committee must, however, request in writing that the accused submit a written explanation in relation to the accusation. That request must be accompanied by a summary of the evidence relating to each alleged offence including additional offences which the Committee is treating as the subject of accusation in view of evidence which has emerged in the course of its investigation.[17] The Committee may proceed to take a decision

---

[10] Ss 6, 8 and 9.
[11] S 9.
[12] S 8.
[13] S 11. The evidence of the additional offence is to be held to constitute an accusation and the accused person, the clerk to the Episcopal Synod and the diocesan Bishop are to be notified accordingly. There is no requirement at this stage to notify the original complainer.
[14] S 10.
[15] S 2(c) – violation of the Canons or of anything lawfully ordered thereunder.
[16] Canon 58.
[17] S 12.

on the accusation in the absence of a written explanation if the accused fails to submit it within the required time.[18]

The Committee, as has been seen, can request an explanation from the accused only after its investigation has been completed. An explanation may, however, reveal matters which call for further investigation. The Canon does not appear to address that issue. If the investigation is reopened, the completion of the previous investigation must be disregarded and, unless the committee finds that no offence has been committed and determines that no further action should be taken, a written explanation must be requested of new on the completion of the reopened investigation.

7.4.2 Decision and disposal by Preliminary Proceedings Committee

Having completed its investigation and considered any written explanations given by the accused and any representations or information supplied by the College of Bishops[19] the decisions which the Committee may competently make are:

(a) to refer the accusation to the Procurator of the Church for trial;

(b) if the accused is not a diocesan Bishop, to refer the accusation to the cleric's diocesan Bishop to issue a warning or advice letter;[20]

(c) to decide that no further action shall be taken; and

(d) to refer the accusation and the results of the investigations to the police or to any other relevant body.[21]

Where the Committee has decided not to refer an accusation for trial but receives within 2 years thereafter a further accusation against the same cleric, it may reconsider the original accusation along with the subsequent one and disregard its earlier decision.[22]

---

[18] S 13.

[19] S 14.

[20] The Bishop is to issue the letter after consultation with the Committee. Any advice given or, in particular, any warning must, it is submitted, avoid proceeding on an assumption that an offence has been committed for that is not a matter for the Committee, or for the Bishop, to decide.

[21] S 15. The wording is such as to enable the Committee to make decisions under more than one of the four listed headings, except that a decision under (c) must clearly stand alone. It is, however, likely that a decision under more than one heading will rarely be appropriate.

7.5   Procedure following Reference for Trial

Once an accusation has been referred to him, it is for the Procurator to decide whether or not to proceed to trial. Before deciding not to proceed he must, however, give notice of his intention to the College of Bishops and take into consideration any view which they may express; and if at any time after referral of an accusation and before the issue of a notice of trial, the College of Bishops request that an accusation should not proceed to trial the Procurator must consider that request before reaching a decision on whether to proceed.[23]

The Canon provides[24] that, the Procurator may require the preliminary proceedings committee to make further investigation or obtain additional information. That is a useful power for assisting the Procurator both in deciding whether to proceed to trial and in preparation for trial. If as a result, evidence is obtained of a further offence relating to a matter in which the Preliminary Proceedings Committee has made a decision, an allegation concerning that offence may be included by the Procurator in the notice of trial notwithstanding that in respect of that allegation no request for a written explanation was made by the Committee. In that event the Procurator is to request a written explanation from the accused and do so, so far as reasonably practicable, at least 1 calendar month before the issue of any notice of trial.

7.6   Notice of Trial and Answers

If the Procurator decides to proceed to trial he must, at least 2 calendar months prior to the trial date, issue a notice to the accused specifying the date and place of trial, the date of issue of the notice, the offence alleged to have been committed and details of date and place and the alleged facts on which the offence is based.[25] Provided those requirements are met, the Procurator may include in the notice an accusation in relation to which no allegation was included in the original accusation and on which no decision was made by the Preliminary Proceedings Committee.[26] This provision is independent of and wider ranging than the provision noted above where evidence of a further offence, relating to a matter in which the Preliminary Proceedings Committee has

---

[22] S 19.
[23] S 22.
[24] S 21 and Form E of Appendix 24.
[25] S 23.
[26] *Ibid.*

made a decision, arises in the course of further investigation. It is difficult to reconcile with the functions the Canon otherwise gives to the Preliminary Proceedings Committee.

Not later than 1 calendar month from the date of issue of the notice of trial, the accused must lodge with the Clerk of the Clergy Discipline Tribunal an answer to the notice specifying whether in relation to each of the accusations he pleads guilty or not guilty and, in relation to any accusation to which he pleads not guilty, the nature of his defence and the facts upon which the defence is based.[27]

The notice of trial requires parties, at least 14 days before the date fixed for trial, to furnish the Clerk of the tribunal and any other party with a list of all the documents on which he proposes to rely and a list of all witnesses whom he proposes to examine.[28] The list of documents must be accompanied by copies of the documents listed. This requirement, although contained in a notice issued by the Procurator, must in equity apply to him as a party as well as to the accused.

7.7 Plea of Guilty

If an accused person pleads guilty, whether in his answers to the notice of trial or by later written intimation, it is for the Procurator to decide whether or not to accept that plea. If he decides to accept it he should lodge a formal acceptance with the Clerk of the tribunal within 7 days of the accused's answer or written intimation and send a copy to the accused.[29] Outstanding accusations in respect of which there has not been a plea of guilty proceed to trial and, in that event, sentence on all accusations is deferred until the trial is concluded.[30] Where, however, after acceptance of a plea of guilty, there are no accusations outstanding against the accused or any co-accused the tribunal should sit within 2 weeks of the date of lodging of the formal acceptance in order to pronounce sentence.[31]

7.8 Abandonment by Procurator

At any time after the lodging of answers by the accused and before the commencement of trial, the Procurator may, in effect,

---

[27] S 24
[28] S 23.
[29] S 25.
[30] S 26.
[31] S 27.

abandon the accusation and he must consider any request to that effect made by the College of Bishops.[32] Abandonment is effected by the Procurator's deciding not to lead evidence.[33] The Canon is silent on the procedure to be followed in the event of such a decision except that the decision must be intimated to the tribunal before evidence is led.[34] Where a decision is made before the tribunal sits it is, it is submitted, appropriate that the decision should be intimated to the Clerk of the tribunal and the accused. The consequence of a decision not to lead evidence must be that when the tribunal sits for trial it should return a verdict of not guilty.

7.9   Trial Sitting: Clergy Discipline Tribunal

All trials take place before a sitting of the Clergy Discipline Tribunal. That tribunal, whose members are appointed for a 3-year term, consists of three practising lawyers of at least 10 years' standing, three clerics from the order of priest or deacon and three communicant lay members of the Church, all appointed by the General Synod, and two bishops appointed by the College of Bishops.[35] A sitting for the purposes of trial consists of three of the Tribunal's members, one being a practising lawyer, another a priest or deacon and the third a lay member.[36] If the accused is a bishop the place of a priest or deacon is taken by a bishop.

7.9.1   Procedure at trial

The trial may be held anywhere in Scotland and should be held in public unless the Tribunal determines otherwise.[37]

Procedure at the trial, in so far as not already provided for in the Canon, is to be governed by rules made by the Clergy Discipline Tribunal and in all matters not otherwise specified in those rules by the Rules of the Court of Session currently in force.[38] No rules to govern its own proceedings have, however, yet been made by

[32] S 29. There is a hiatus in the Canon in that it provides no procedure for abandonment or for a request by the College of Bishops between the issuing of the notice of trial by the Procurator and the lodging of answers by the accused.
[33] S 28.
[34] Ibid.
[35] S 31.
[36] S 33(a) and (d). The President of the Tribunal determines which members should sit and also which member should preside.
[37] S 34.
[38] S 32

the Tribunal.[39] The result is that at present, except where there is express canonical provision or the Rules of the Court of Session are applicable, the conduct of any proceedings is, subject to the principles of natural justice, at the discretion of the trial tribunal. The only canonical provisions affecting procedure, apart from those already noticed, are those dealing with certain questions of evidence mentioned in the next paragraph.

7.9.2 Evidence

Where evidence is led it should be recorded in such way as the Tribunal may direct.[40] The Tribunal may accept a conviction of the accused of a criminal offence by a secular court as sufficient evidence of the fact that the accused committed the offence provided that, before the Tribunal accepts the conviction as conclusive, the accused has had an opportunity to adduce evidence. The Tribunal may accept as evidence a duly authenticated record of evidence given in any court of the United Kingdom in any cause affecting the accused.[41] Subject to those provisions and such provisions of the Rules of the Court of Session as bear on questions of evidence the Tribunal has the same discretion in relation to matters of evidence as it has in procedural matters generally. It might be thought, from the assimilation of procedure under the Canon to civil procedure, that the Scottish law of evidence, as used in the secular courts for civil proceedings, should apply but there is nothing, as matters stand, to oblige the Tribunal to follow that course except insofar as the Rules of Court so require. The burden of proof lies, it is submitted, on the Procurator.[42] The standard of proof is not laid down but it may be inferred that it is on a balance of probabilities. That can be justified on the view that, despite some quasi-criminal features, the proceedings are essentially civil in character and that their purpose is not punitive but the achievement of a just solution in the interests of the whole Church. It remains, however, right for the Tribunal to take the gravity of the accusation into account in determining whether the burden of proof has been discharged.

---

[39] Draft rules have been prepared but at the time of writing there is no indication of when they will be finalised and published.

[40] S 34.

[41] Ibid.

[42] This follows from the ordinary rules of civil procedure and from the scheme of the Canon. There may, however, be circumstances in which an evidential burden passes to the accused.

7.9.3 *Verdict*

In respect of each accusation the trial tribunal may return a verdict, which may be unanimous or by a majority, finding the accused guilty or not guilty. The Tribunal may retire to consider its verdict which it may give either on the last day of the trial or at a later date.[43] Reasons must be given for the verdict and a written copy of the verdict and reasons must be sent to each accused person and to the Procurator.[44]

7.9.4 *Sentence*

The sentences open to the Tribunal in the event of a finding of guilty on any charge are:

    (a) absolute discharge;
    (b) rebuke;
    (c) injunction to perform or refrain from performing a specified act or acts;
    (d) removal from office;
    (e) disqualification from holding office;
    (f) prohibition from the exercise of the ministry of Bishop, Priest or Deacon.

Provided there is no essential inconsistency in doing so, the Tribunal may pronounce one or more of the above sentences in respect of any charge as its thinks fit.[45]

7.10 Appeals

A cleric convicted of any accusation may appeal against verdict or sentence on the ground of miscarriage of justice in the proceedings, including miscarriage on the basis of error of law, unreasonable finding of fact made by the trial tribunal or additional evidence the existence and significance of which was

---

[43] S 35.
[44] S 37.
[45] S 36. Where the accused is removed from office, disqualified from holding office, or prohibited from the exercise of holy orders he has no right or claim to any income from any offices held at the date of sentence or to perform the duties pertaining to them and is required to vacate any property occupied by reason of office within 3 months from that date. In cases falling within (e) or (f) above the accused may apply, after the lapse of 3 years, to the College of Bishops for restoration of the capacity to hold office or exercise a ministry.

not available and could not reasonably have been made available at the trial.[46] Questions of whether the sentence was excessive, oppressive or inappropriate may, it is submitted, be included in what may amount to a miscarriage of justice for the purposes of an appeal against sentence. The individual grounds of appeal should be stated in a note of appeal sent to the Clerk of the Tribunal and received by him within 21 days of sentence being passed. Failure to send the note timeously entails loss of the right to appeal.

Appeals are heard before five members of the Clergy Discipline Tribunal, one being a practising lawyer, two being clerics from the order of Priest or Deacon and another two being members of the laity. Where the appellant is a Bishop one of the clerics is replaced by a member of the Tribunal who is a Bishop.[47] Having heard an appeal against conviction, the Tribunal may:

(a) affirm the verdict and uphold the conviction;
(b) set aside the verdict and cancel the sentence;
(c) affirm the sentence;
(d) set aside the sentence and substitute an amended sentence, whether more or less severe.[48]

There is no power to affirm or set aside a verdict only in part. The appeal tribunal may, however, in giving reasons for its decision to uphold a conviction, indicate any points of difference it has from the trial tribunal's reasons or findings in fact and that difference of opinion may be reflected in the appeal tribunal's decision on sentence.

Clearly, the Tribunal can affirm a sentence under (c) above or substitute an amended sentence under (d) only if the conviction is upheld. The Canon bears at this point to apply only to appeals against conviction and fails to indicate how the Tribunal is to dispose of an appeal against sentence alone, but it is submitted that, despite the apparent *lacuna*, (c) and (d) above must be held to apply to appeals against sentence alone as well as to the consequences for sentence of the Tribunal's decision on the merits of an appeal against conviction.

The judgment of the Tribunal on an appeal should be made in respect of each individual ground of appeal and may be

---

[46] S 38.
[47] S 33(b) and (c).
[48] S 38.

unanimous or by a majority. It may be made on the last day of the appeal hearing or at a later date. A copy of the written judgment should be sent to each appellant and to the Procurator.[49] Where a sentence is cancelled (and the verdict set aside) under (b) above the Tribunal may order a retrial. In that event a new notice of trial must be sent to the accused within 2 months of the order for retrial.[50]

7.11   Suspension from Office Pending Proceedings

Where the Preliminary Proceedings Committee makes a decision to refer an accusation for trial to the Procurator or to refer an accusation and the results of its investigations to the police or to any other relevant public body, the accused cleric is automatically suspended from office pending the outcome of proceedings. The same result follows, but at the time of the lodging of the accusation, where the Provincial Officer for the Protection of Children and Vulnerable Adults lodges an accusation alleging the abuse of children or vulnerable adults.[51] In any other circumstances it is for the diocesan Bishop to consider, when an accusation is lodged, whether to suspend the accused cleric from office[52] and, if the accused cleric is a diocesan Bishop, it is competent for the Primus, at any time after an accusation is lodged, to make an order, subject to appeal to the Episcopal Synod, suspending the Bishop from office.[53] Suspension is without loss of emoluments and the accused cleric is entitled to continue to reside in any accommodation provided for him unless, given the location of the accommodation and the nature of the accusation, the diocesan Bishop requires him to reside in alternative accommodation.[54]

---

[49] S 39.
[50] S 38.
[51] S 18.
[52] Ibid.
[53] Canon 6, s 9.
[54] Canon 54, s 18 and Canon 6, s 9.

CHAPTER 8

A NOTE ON ROMAN CATHOLIC CANON LAW

FRANCIS GILL, WS

8.1 Introduction

The internal law of the Roman Catholic Church is set out comprehensively in the Code of Canon Law. Reflecting the universality of the Church, the Code applies to all Roman Catholics throughout the world and does not allow for any local deviations.

The Canon Law was codified in 1917. The second, and current, Code was promulgated in 1983.[1]

8.2 The Scottish National Tribunal

In Scotland all ecclesiastical disputes that cannot be resolved by a Bishop at a local level and that involve issues of canon law will normally be referred to the Scottish National Tribunal[2] which is situated in Glasgow. It is staffed by full-time and part-time priests qualified in canon law who are appointed by the Bishops' Conference of Scotland. The senior post is that of President or *officialis*. The Scottish National Tribunal was established in 1970. Its first *officialis* was the late Cardinal Thomas Joseph Winning, Archbishop of Glasgow between 1974 and 2001.

The Scottish National Tribunal is categorised as a Regional Tribunal. Domestic tribunals in the different dioceses throughout the world have their own written constitutions which deal most importantly with the scope of their jurisdiction. The Scottish National Tribunal is a tribunal *pro universis causis*. It is a tribunal of first instance. Scottish cases that are appealed are

---

[1] *Codex Iuris Canonici.*
[2] The Scottish National Tribunal, 22 Woodrow Road, Glasgow G41 5PN.

dealt with by the Tribunal of the Archdiocese of Birmingham. Third-instance cases are remitted to the Church's highest judicial body, the *Signatura Apostolica* in Rome, although, with the permission of the *Signatura*, such cases can be dealt with in special circumstances by the Tribunals of either Dublin or Westminster. All of the judges of the Scottish National Tribunal at the present time are ordained clergy with the requisite qualifications in Canon Law. They are drawn from each of the eight dioceses in Scotland. Most of the work of the Tribunal concerns marriage cases. More than 100 of these are accepted for formal investigation each year. The Tribunal processes cases involving all marriages and not just marriages involving Catholics. This might seem strange when the Code governs only people of the Latin Rite. However, in some cases the Church has an interest in investigating the validity of a marriage of a non-Catholic who may wish to marry a Catholic.

Other forms of actions include petitions for dispensation from the obligations of priesthood. The Tribunal has been given competence by the Vatican to hear all canonical and judicial matters including formal cases and summary cases decided on documents only, as well as contentious cases. Complaints against Bishops are, however, reserved to the jurisdiction of the Sacred Congregation for Bishops. His Holiness the Pope is judicially immune.

It will be rare for a civil lawyer to appear before a canon law tribunal in Scotland. This contrasts with the position in, for example, Italy and Spain where it is common for civil lawyers to conduct hearings before canon law tribunals. The principal reason is that most ecclesiastical disputes are capable of resolution without recourse to a tribunal. Often civil lawyers will become involved in that process, but such matters are generally decided with regard to the civil law and not the Code of Canon Law.

The second reason is that it is difficult on a practical level for a lay Roman Catholic to obtain a formal qualification in the subject. While the Canon Law Society of Great Britain and Ireland[3] exists to promote the study of and interest in the canon law of the Roman Catholic Church, its membership is made up almost entirely of ordained clergy or religious. Membership of the Society is at the discretion of the officers and committee of the Society. It is not possible to study for a qualification in canon law in the United Kingdom on a part-time basis or by distance learning.

---

[3] www.clsgbi.org.

8.3 Cases brought to the Tribunal

Where an individual member of the Church or priest does wish to take the matter to a tribunal then, following guidance from the Bishop or from the Tribunal itself, the applicant will appoint an advocate to conduct the case before that tribunal. The advocate (in this context not a member of the Faculty of Advocates) will be qualified in canon law and experienced in presenting cases in that forum.

In Scotland, the civil law regards the Tribunal as having privative jurisdiction within the limits of its own constitution in questions affecting individual members, the rationale being that the members have voluntarily submitted themselves to the constitution and rules of the Church.

While the Scottish courts respect the jurisdiction of the tribunals of the Church in matters of ecclesiastical discipline, they will hold decisions of those tribunals to be of no effect in the eyes of the civil law where the tribunal has exceeded its jurisdiction, or where the proceedings were irregular, or where the decision was irrational or contrary to natural justice.

Sadly, the Roman Catholic Church in recent times has been involved in civil court cases throughout the United Kingdom concerning "historical abuse". In the main these arose out of alleged abuse of minors in certain residential homes run by religious orders and where local clergy, often including the bishop, were appointed to the Board of Managers. These claims, although involving usually both a priest as the defender and a member of the Church as the pursuer, did not require any detailed analysis of the Code of Canon Law. In some cases, however, canonical penalties such as compulsory laicisation were imposed on some of the priests involved although not those who were simply brought into the case because of their role on the Board of Managers.

In recent years a number of internal disputes in the Catholic Church have surfaced in the civil courts and tribunals in the form of claims for unfair dismissal, petitions for interdict and the like. This seems to be an emerging trend in Churches of different denominations throughout the United Kingdom.

APPENDIX

STANDING ORDERS OF THE GENERAL ASSEMBLY
(excerpt)

V. CONDUCT OF CASES

56. **Commission of Assembly.** In Sections 57–59 references to the General Assembly shall be taken to refer where appropriate to the Commission of Assembly and all references shall be so construed *mutatis mutandis.*

(a) Lodging of papers

57. **Appeal; Dissent and Complaint; Petition.** The papers in all cases intended to be brought before the Assembly, whether Appeals or Dissents and Complaints against the judgement of inferior courts, or Petitions, should be lodged with the Clerks of Assembly not later than 24 April, and must be lodged not less than fourteen days before the opening session of Assembly; except in the case of judgements pronounced within sixteen days of the meeting of Assembly, in which case they shall be lodged within forty-eight hours of the judgement being pronounced.

58(a). **Reference.** In the case of Reference of a matter from an inferior court for the judgement of the Assembly the same limits as to time for lodging of papers in the case shall apply as in SO 57.

(b). **Reference of Matter Previously Considered.** Where the matter of a Reference has previously been under consideration of the Assembly, the Reference shall state the date when the matter was previously before the Assembly and shall narrate the Assembly's Deliverance thereon.

59. **Answers.** It shall be competent for all parties claiming an interest in the subject matter of an Appeal, Dissent and Complaint or Petition to lodge Answers thereto complying

with the requirements of SO 60. Answers may be lodged any time after the Appeal, Dissent and Complaint or Petition is received by the Clerks, but not later than seven days before the opening meeting of Assembly. Answers shall be in the form of articulate numbered Answers to the narrative contained in the Appeal, Dissent and Complaint or Petition, indicating in particular matters of fact that are admitted and denied, and shall set forth a concise statement of the Respondent's case, together with a crave specifying the action the Assembly are invited to take thereanent.

(b) Printing of papers

60. **Printing.** It shall be the duty of the Clerks on receiving papers that are to come before the Assembly in connection with cases to arrange to have these printed in authorised form, stitched together and paged.

61. **In Private.** Papers relating to business dealt with by Presbyteries in private, or which the Committee on Overtures and Cases (SO 6) consider should be taken in private, shall be printed separately and may be dealt with by the Assembly in private.

62. **Cost of Printing.** In cases of discipline brought before the Assembly by the Judicial Commission, by Reference from a Presbytery, or by complaint by a minority of the Court, the expense of printing shall be borne by the Assembly Arrangements Committee; in other circumstances by the Complainer or Appellant. In all other cases the expense of printing in sufficient numbers for the use of Commissioners shall be borne by the party having interest in the same or desiring a Deliverance from the Assembly.

63. *In Retentis.* Two copies of every printed paper shall be kept by the Clerks of Assembly to be bound up and retained among the Records of Assembly.

(c) Circulation of papers

64. **Date of Dispatch.** A copy of all papers transmitted to the Clerks of Assembly not later than 24 April shall be forwarded by them to each Member of Assembly at least one week before the opening day of the Assembly.

65. **In Private.** The Clerks of Assembly shall not issue in advance to Members the papers in cases which they think require

to be conducted in private, until specially instructed by the Assembly so to do; but shall report such cases to the Convener of the Business Committee, for the information of that Committee, immediately after its appointment.

(d) Intimation to parties

66. **Appeal; Dissent and Complaint.** In all cases coming before the Assembly by Appeal or Dissent and Complaint it shall be the duty of the Clerks of Assembly to inform the parties on both sides as soon as possible of the time at which such case is likely to be taken by the Assembly. Such intimation shall, unless in a specific case the Assembly determine otherwise, be regarded as sufficient notice.

The Clerks shall further be bound, on application made to them for the purpose, to supply six copies of all prints made in pursuance of the foregoing Orders to the opposite party or parties in any case, or to his or their duly accredited Agents.

67. **Petition.** In every Petition it shall be the duty of the Petitioner to make such intimation of the Petition as may be necessary having regard to the nature of the Petition. Such intimation shall be made not more than seven days later than the time when the Petition is lodged with the Clerks of Assembly as provided in SO 57 above; and along with the Petition there shall be lodged a certificate signed by the Petitioner or his or her Agent setting forth the names of the parties to whom such intimation has been made or is to be made. The Assembly may refuse to dispose of any Petition if in their opinion sufficient intimation thereof has not been made.

(e) Transmission to Assembly

68. **Committee on Overtures and Cases.** All papers lodged with the Clerks in cases of every sort in terms of the foregoing Orders shall be laid by them before the Committee on Overtures and Cases, which shall consider the same and report to the Assembly.

69. **Decision not to Transmit.** If the Committee on Overtures and Cases shall decide not to transmit to the Assembly any papers in cases duly lodged with the Clerks of Assembly it shall report the same to the Assembly at their first Session, or at the Session next after such decision, with its reasons for not transmitting the papers, and parties shall be entitled

to be heard thereon at the bar of the Assembly. Intimation of a decision not to transmit papers shall be made to the parties concerned as soon as possible, and in time to allow of their being represented at the bar when the decision not to transmit is reported to the Assembly.

70. **In Private.** The Business Committee shall, in its first Report, specify any case which in its judgement requires to be conducted in private, and any case which does not appear to it to be of that character although the Clerks of Assembly may have reported it as such. The Assembly shall thereupon determine by a special Deliverance, at what stage in the proceedings the papers in such a case shall be issued to the Commissioners. In every case which the Assembly appoint to be conducted in private the instruction to issue the papers shall be accompanied by a special exhortation to the Commissioners to keep them private.

71. **Proposed Legislation.** All Overtures from Presbyteries or from Commissioners which propose the introduction of new or the amendment of existing Acts (or Regulations) shall contain the precise terms of the legislation which they propose; and the Committee on Overtures and Cases shall not transmit to the Assembly any Overture which is deficient in this respect, provided always that the Clerks and Procurator shall be available to assist with the framing of such proposals.

(f) Hearing of cases

72. **Announcement.** Before parties are heard in any contentious case the Clerk shall read the following announcement, *viz* – "The Commissioners are reminded that justice requires that all the pleadings at the bar should be heard by all those who vote in this case, and that their judgement should be made solely on the basis of the pleadings." Immediately before a vote is taken in such a case, the Clerk shall read the following further announcement, *viz* – "The Commissioners are reminded that only those who have heard all the pleadings at the bar are entitled to vote in this case."

73. **Appeal; Complaint; One Appellant.** In cases brought before the Assembly by Appeal, where there is only one appellant (or one set of appellants concurring in the same reasons of Appeal) and only one respondent (or one set of respondents

concurring in the same answers to the reasons of Appeal) the case for the appellant (or set of appellants) shall be stated by him or herself or by his or her counsel, who at the same time shall submit such argument upon the case as he or she shall think fit. The party or counsel so stating the Appeal shall be followed by the respondent or his or her counsel who likewise shall submit such arguments upon the case as he or she shall think fit. At the close of the statement for the respondent the appellant shall be entitled to be again heard, and the respondent shall also be entitled to be heard in answer to the second speech for the appellant and if, in his or her final answer, the respondent shall state any fact or submit any argument not adverted to in his or her answer to the opening statement for the appellant, the appellant shall be entitled to a reply upon the new matter introduced in the final answer for the respondent. With the exception of this right of reply, so limited, more than two speeches shall not be allowed to any party at the bar.

74. **Appeal; Complaint; More than one Appellant.** In such cases as those referred to in SO 73 if there is more than one appellant (or set of appellants) insisting on the Appeal, or more than one respondent (or set of respondents) supporting the judgement appealed against, (a) on different grounds, or (b) in separate reasons or answers, each appellant shall be entitled to open and state his separate case, and each respondent shall be entitled to make his or her separate answer, and the debate shall be closed with a reply for the several appellants; provided always that it shall be competent to the parties, with consent of the Assembly to make any arrangement for conducting the debate other than herein prescribed, if it shall have the effect of limiting, further than is herein done, the number of speeches to be made from the bar.

75. **Appeal; Complaint; Who may appear.** Any Member of an inferior court whose judgement is brought under review of the Assembly may appear at the bar in support of the judgement; but, when Commissioners have been specially appointed by the inferior court to support its judgement, the Assembly shall not hear any Member of such court other than the Commissioners so appointed, unless any Member not so appointed but wishing to be heard can show a separate and peculiar interest to support the judgement; and in all such cases it shall be competent to the Assembly

to limit the number of Members of an inferior court who shall be heard in support of the judgement under review.

76. **Dissents and Complaints.** In SO 73 to 75, "Appeal" includes "Dissents and Complaints" and "Appellant" includes "Complainer".

77. **Petition.** In cases brought before the Assembly as the court of first instance by Petition, the party promoting the application shall be entitled to be heard in support of the same; and the Assembly shall also hear an answer from any party at the bar claiming to be heard whom it shall consider to be a proper respondent, and the debate at the bar shall be closed with a reply from the person promoting the application.

78. **Reference.** In cases brought before the Assembly by reference from a Presbytery the reference shall be stated to the Assembly by a Member of the referring court, specially appointed for the purpose, at the bar if not a Commissioner, or in his or her place as a Commissioner if a Commissioner from the Presbytery. The Assembly shall thereafter hear the parties in the case referred in such order as the nature of the case may seem to require, keeping in view the regulations in SO 73 to 78.

79. **Readjustment Cases.** In cases arising from Act VII 2003, when a request for determination follows a decision of the Committee on Parish Appraisal not to concur in the judgement of a Presbytery, the Convener, or other member of the said Committee, shall be heard at the bar if not a Commissioner, or in his or her place as a Commissioner if a Commissioner, immediately after the request for determination has been stated. After the initial statement, and the response by the said Committee when applicable, the General Assembly shall hear at the bar such parties in the case as are not represented by Commissioners, in such order as the nature of the case may seem to require.

VI. ORDER OF DEBATE

(a) Order of the day

80. When the Assembly have resolved that a case or other piece of business shall be taken up at a certain hour mentioned in the Order of Business, such case or other piece of business shall be taken not later than the hour

fixed and the business before the Assembly, if not finished
at the hour named, shall be adjourned, provided that, in
the case of an Order of the Day following the Report of
the Church and Society Council, such unfinished business
shall not be taken up. If, in the opinion of the Moderator,
it would be in accordance with the general convenience of
the Assembly, the Moderator may allow the transaction
of the business then actually under discussion to continue
for a period of not more than fifteen minutes beyond the
specified time, but no fresh business shall be commenced.

(b) Motions

81. **Right to Move.** Any Commissioner to the Assembly may
make a motion upon any matter coming regularly before
the Assembly; and on rising to do so he or she shall read
the terms of the motion having wherever possible handed
the same in writing on the form provided to the Assembly
Office or other point of collection intimated to the General
Assembly. It shall be in order to move a motion regarding
any matter in the care of a Committee to which no reference
is made in the Report of that Committee, provided that
reasonable notice has been given in writing to the Convener
before presentation of the Report. The mover of any
counter-motion or amendment may reply to the discussion
of his or her motion, immediately before the Convener
closes the debate.

82. **Withdrawal.** When a motion has been duly seconded it shall
not be competent to withdraw it, or to make any alteration
upon it, without the permission of the Assembly.

83. **Priority.** The Deliverance on the Report of a Committee
shall take precedence of any other motion on that subject.

84. **Committee Convener.** The Convener of a Committee
when a Commissioner, on giving in the Report of that
Committee, shall move the Deliverance proposed in terms
of SO 40. A Convener, when not a Commissioner, shall be
allowed to submit the Report of the Committee, and to give
explanations in the subsequent discussion. In such a case
the Principal Clerk, whom failing, the Depute Clerk, shall
formally move the Deliverance. In all cases the Convener
shall have the right of replying to the debate.

85. **Introducer of Overture.** The Introducer of an Overture, if a
Commissioner, shall move the Deliverance; and if he or she

is not a Commissioner the Principal Clerk, whom failing the Depute Clerk, shall formally move the Deliverance. The Introducer, whether a Commissioner or not, may answer questions or give explanations in the course of the debate and, if a Commissioner, may reply to, the discussion immediately before the relevant Convener closes the debate.

86. **Notice of Motion.** Any Commissioner may, during the sittings of the Assembly, give notice of Motion on any subject due to come regularly before the Assembly, other than a contentious case. Notices of Motion so given in shall be printed in the "Assembly Papers" not later than the day before that on which the business is to be taken. Such printed Notice of Motion shall confer no right of priority of moving same, the Moderator being the sole judge of the order in which Members are entitled to address the Assembly.

(c) **The debate**

87. **The Chair.** Every speaker shall address the Assembly through the Moderator, and the correct address is "Moderator".

88. **In Support.** When a motion or motions have been made and seconded, any Member (including a formal seconder in terms of SO 92) may take part in subsequent debate.

89. **One Speech only.** Except as provided in SO 84, no Member may speak twice on the same matter except in explanation, and then only by special permission of the Assembly.

90. **Point of Order.** Any Member may rise to speak to a Point of Order. A speaker is not to be interrupted unless upon a call to order. When so interrupted he or she shall cease speaking, and shall resume his or her seat until the Point of Order is decided. The Member calling to order shall state the grounds for so doing; and the speaker who has been interrupted may briefly reply in explanation, to show that he or she is not out of order, but no other Member may speak to the Point of Order unless with the permission or at the request of the Moderator, with whom the decision of the point rests, though the Moderator may put the point to a vote of the Assembly.

91. There shall be no right of reply to a debate except as provided for by SO 81 and 84.

92. **Limits.** All speeches shall be limited to 5 minutes, with the following exceptions:

(i) Committees
Convener giving in the Report of his or her Committee and moving thereon
(seconding to be formal)   20 minutes

Movers of Amendments or Counter-Motions
(seconding to be formal)   10 minutes

(ii) Overtures
Introducing an Overture and when the Introducer is a
Commissioner, moving thereon   10 minutes
Mover of other Motions in relation to Overture
(seconding to be formal)   5 minutes

(iii) Petitions
Speeches of Petitioners   10 minutes

93. **No Time Limit.** The time limits shall apply, except in the following cases:

(a) when the Assembly are debating specific proposals for change under Barrier Act procedure;
(b) when the Assembly are exercising judicial functions;
(c) in Petitions when, for special reasons, the Committee on Overtures and Cases reports that the circumstances demand an extension, and when the General Assembly adopt that opinion;
(d) in any other matter when the Assembly Arrangements Committee (in respect of the Order of Business for the first two days) or the Business Committee (in respect of the Order of Business for the subsequent days) declares that, in its opinion, such matter is of exceptional importance, and when the Assembly adopt that opinion.

(d) Dealing with motions

94. **Character of Motions.** Motions shall be considered as belonging to one of the following categories, and shall be dealt with as prescribed, *viz*:

1. The original Motion.
2. Counter-Motions – being Motions contradictory or negative of the original Motion or of a substantial part of the original Motion.

3. Amendments being Motions not substantially contradictory of the original Motion or Counter-Motion, but for making deletions, alterations, or additions thereto without defeating its main object.

4. Amendments of amendments already moved and seconded.

95. **Moderator to Judge.** The Moderator shall be judge of the category to which any Motions shall be considered to belong, and the ruling of the Moderator shall be final.

96. **Grouping of Amendments.** When to any Proposed Deliverance there has been given notice of amendments which differ from each other only slightly in their general tenor, the Moderator shall decide whether or not to permit more than one of such amendments to be moved.

97. **Voting on Amendments.** When an amendment (Category 3) has been proposed it shall be disposed of by the Assembly before any other counter-motion or amendment is proposed. However, it shall be in order for an amendment of an amendment (Category 4) to be proposed, seconded and debated, after which the Moderator shall take a vote "For" or "Against". When all such Category 4 motions have been so disposed of, the Assembly shall complete its consideration of the original amendment (Category 3) and the Moderator shall take a vote "For" or "Against" the original amendment amended or unamended as the case may be. For the avoidance of doubt, it is affirmed that the order of debate for Category 3 and Category 4 motions shall be the same except as herein provided and that the provisions of SO 84 shall apply to both.

98. **Voting on Motions.** After all amendments, if any, have been disposed of, the Moderator shall take a vote between all Motions in Categories (l) and (2), and in doing so shall adopt the following procedure. A vote shall be taken in one of the methods provided below, between all the Motions in the order in which they were made, beginning at the first. Each Commissioner may vote for one Motion only. If, on the numbers being announced, one Motion has obtained a clear majority of votes, all the other Motions shall fall; but if no Motion has obtained a clear majority, the Motion having the smallest number of votes shall be struck off and a vote taken between the remaining Motions; and the Assembly may determine.

99. **Voting for Appointments.** In the case of voting for appointments to vacant offices in the Church, where there are more than two nominations the Assembly shall vote separately on all the names proposed, and, unless there be a majority in favour of one over all the others combined, the one having the lowest number shall be dropped, and the Assembly shall again vote on those that remain.

100. **Deliberative Vote.** The Moderator or Acting Moderator in the Chair shall have no Deliberative Vote.

101. **Casting Vote.** If in any division there shall be an equality of votes for two proposals before the Assembly, the Moderator shall have power to give a deciding vote; and if in the course of the voting as provided in SO 98 and 99 above, there should be an equality of votes for the two Motions having fewest votes, the Moderator shall have power to give a deciding vote and the Motion for which the Moderator shall vote shall be retained for the purpose of the next vote of the Assembly.

(e) **Taking the vote**

102. **Vote by Standing.** The Moderator may, if so minded, ascertain the mind of the Assembly by asking the Commissioners to stand in their places, and shall intimate to the Assembly on which side there is in his or her opinion a majority. Unless the opinion of the Moderator so intimated is at once challenged it shall become the decision of the Assembly. If any Commissioner challenge the opinion of the Moderator the Assembly shall proceed to take a Vote by Electronic System as provided in SO 103.

103. **Voting by Electronic System.** If the Moderator is not prepared to give an opinion on the result of a vote by standing, or if his or her opinion is challenged, and whenever the Assembly are hearing a case, the Assembly shall proceed to take a vote by electronic system, using a system approved by the Assembly Arrangements Committee. The Business Committee shall ensure that Commissioners are familiar with the method of a vote by electronic system and may appoint tellers to assist Commissioners with the process of casting votes. After all votes have been counted the Moderator shall intimate the result of the voting. In no circumstances shall a second vote be taken on a matter which has already been the subject of a vote by electronic system.

(f) Dissents

104. **Entering.** Any Commissioner dissatisfied with a judgement of the Assembly, which has not been unanimous, has the right to enter his or her dissent against it; but no dissent can be given in until the matter to which it refers has, for that session, been disposed of, the Minute adjusted, and the Assembly is ready to proceed to other business.

105. **Adhering.** When a dissent has been entered, it is in order for any other Commissioner present when that judgement was pronounced to adhere to such dissent. No other's adherence may be entered.

106. **Reasons.** A person dissenting may do so with or without giving in reasons of dissent. If he or she dissent for reasons given in at the time, or to be afterwards given in, such reasons shall, if received by the Assembly as proper and relevant, and provided they are given in before the close of the next session (or, when made on the last day of the Assembly, before the close of the same session), be recorded in the Minutes.

107. **Answers.** If the Assembly appoint a Committee to prepare answers to reasons of dissent, the Report of the Committee shall, except on the last day of the Assembly, be printed in the "Assembly Papers"; and, as approved by the Assembly, shall be printed in the Minutes, if the reasons of dissent have been so printed.

108. **Record of Dissents.** Reasons of dissent and answers thereto when not entered in the Minutes, shall be kept in a separate Record of Dissents.

BIBLIOGRAPHY

Church of Scotland

Burleigh, J H S, *A Church History of Scotland* (Hope Trust: Edinburgh, 1983)

Cheyne, A C, *The Ten Years' Conflict and the Disruption: An Overview* (Scottish Academic Press: Edinburgh, 1993)

Cox, J T, *Practice and Procedure in the Church of Scotland* (Church of Scotland: Edinburgh, 6th edn, 1976), p 201

Herron, A, *The Law and Practice of the Kirk* (Chapterhouse: Glasgow, 1995)

Lyall, F, *Of Presbyters and Kings: Church and State in the Law of Scotland* (AUP: Aberdeen, 1980)

MacLean, M A, *The Crown Rights of the Redeemer: The Spiritual Freedom of the Church of Scotland* (Saint Andrew Press: Edinburgh, 2009)

McGillivray, A G, *An Introduction to Practice and Procedure in the Church of Scotland*: http://www.churchofscotland.org.uk/extranet/xchurchlaw/xchurchlawpracproc.htm

Murray, D M, *Freedom to Reform: The Articles Declaratory of the Church of Scotland 1921* (The Chalmers Lectures of 1991) (T&T Clark: London, 1993)

——, *Rebuilding the Kirk: Presbyterian Reunion in Scotland 1909–1929* (Scottish Academic Press: Edinburgh, 2000)

Rodger of Earlsferry, Lord, *The Courts, the Church and the Constitution: Aspects of the Disruption of 1843* (The Jean Clark Memorial Lectures) (Edinburgh University Press, Edinburgh, 2008)

Weatherhead, J L, (ed), *The Constitution and Laws of the Church of Scotland* (Board of Practice and Procedure, Edinburgh, 1997)

Scottish Episcopal Church

Brodie, P, and Mackay of Clashfern, Lord, "Voluntary Churches" in *Stair Memorial Encyclopedia of the Laws of Scotland*, vol 3, pp 779–801, paras 1632–1653

Wilkinson, A B, "The Scottish Episcopal Church" in *Stair Memorial Encyclopedia of the Laws of Scotland*, vol 3, pp 764–779, paras 1610–1631

INDEX

libel, trial by, 33–34
Lords of the Congregation, 1

manse, vacation of, 41
marriage cases
    Scottish National Tribunal, 84
Medical Review Panel
    appeal from, 63
    assessment procedure, 62
    decision, 62–63
    referral to, 61–62
mental incapacity of clergy, 61–64
ministers (Church of Scotland)
    accommodation of, 41
    censure of, 40–41
    discipline of
        generally, 18–19
        procedure, 33–42
    election, 3
    induction, 3, 7
    ordination, 7
    removal of status as, 40
    removal from charge, 17–18
    reprimand of, 40
    suspension of, 40–41
Ministries Appeal Panel, 19–20
Moderator
    addressing, 30–31
    bowing to, 30
    Church of Scotland courts, 8–9
    Commission of Assembly, 15
motions
    adjusting other motions, 22–23
    Commission of Assembly, before, 16
    counter-motions, 22–23
    debate on, 22–24
    disciplinary matters, in, 38–39

natural justice, 27
natural law, 53
non-contested business
    procedure in, 22–25
notice of intention, 58–59
notice of trial, 76–77

offences (SEC), 71–72
ordination
    deacons, of, 7
    elders, of, 2
    ministers, of, 7
Overtures
    10–11
    24–25

"parish appraisal", 14
pastoral breakdown, situations of,
    inquiry into (Scottish Episcopal
    Church), 58–61
pastoral tie, dissolution of (Church of
    Scotland)
    generally, 17–18
    suspension or removal of status,
        following, 40–41
Percy, Miss Helen, 34
Petitions
    11
    24–25
physical incapacity of clergy, 61–64
pleadings, 25
Police Act 1997, 74
Pope, The, judicial immunity of,
    84
prayers, opening and closing, 30
Prelacy Act 1689, 43
Preliminary Proceedings Committee
    decision, 75
    generally, 73
    investigation, 73–75
Presbyterial Commission
    censures imposed by, 40–41
    composition of, 37–38
    decision, 40
    history, 33–34
Presbyterian governance, 1–12
Presbyterianism
    appeals from, 7
    democracy and, 2–3
    governance, 1–12
    reformed polity and, 1–3
    today, 2
Presbytery
    appeals
        from, 6, 7, 11
        to, 7
    clerks to, 9–10
    commissions to, 7–8
    Committees, 8
    court, as, 7–8
    disciplinary matters, role in, 33–42
    minister
        election of, 3
        relationship with, 8
    Moderator, 9
    superintendent function, 7
Presbytery Clerks, 9–10
priesthood obligations, dispensation
    from, 84